MW01230638

THE CIVIL RIGHTS OF BLACK THEOLOGY

Inspired Inspirations for Black Living

Sufficient is thine arm alone.

ISBN: 9798732303407
Copyright © 2021 J.O. Gatson, Th.M

Cover design by: Nspireme2bpublications
Published by NspireMe2B Publications
www.nspiredauthor.com
Nspireme2bpublications@gmail.com
Birmingham, Alabama 35242

O God, our help in ages past, our hope for years to come.

DEDICATION

The published manuscripts for this book has been fully dedicated to my wife, Gloria Williams Gatson, a most purpose driven woman, who has given her life and lifestyle for the mentoring of deserving youth. Likewise, she afforded me personal liberties for executing the completion of this book. Many countless days and nights, she allowed me to author this book without any personal time restraints. Through the dedication of this book and without reservations, we salute her with complete reverence.

J.O. GATSON

Mourn for the thousands slain.

TABLE OF CONTENTS

Help me walk from day to day, With it shadow o'er me.

FOREWORD

The author conveys the intended purpose of this book and the material thereof in a most orthodox way of making the reader apply thought to the prescribed precepts of the book. The literary style poses thought provoking concepts, which motivates one to search even the more, concerning the personal variances of life. It is most obvious, people of color are the intended audience as readers engulf themselves into the presented language and literary style.

Definitely, there is a hidden dialogue between the author, reader and one's state of mind and Spirit. The perceived intent is to strengthen the lives of Believers in the midst of their everyday walk with the Lord, while coping with the assaulting tidal waves of what is known as life. Perhaps, through the worth of the conveyed contents, an unbeliever will become motivated enough to survey his or her own life, per their personal beliefs in the Lord.

The author does his best to permeate a vivid textual writing, which affects all our personal lives day-to-day in various ways. The empowerment from his Soul to the hearts of readers, will allow the readers to lift the text from the pages, while making daily applications to their living experiences.

In closing, this book should be labeled as a self-help manual for everyday living. Even the more, this book can serve as daily reminder for devotion. Yet, without any reservations, the entitled book, "THE CIVIL RIGHTS OF BLACK THEOLOGY" of inspired inspirations will lead readers to recommend this book to family and friends as a must read.

Gloria Williams Gatson

THE CIVIL RIGHTS OF BLACK THEOLOGY

Inspired Inspirations for Black Living

Jesus knows our every weakness.

LITERARY DISCLOSURE

This book has been intentionally composed and written by design with a grammatical type language usage and style which directs a presupposed literary style for predominantly African American readers. This includes readers of other backgrounds and cultures. Inclusively, to supersede the rules of grammar analysis at all levels. Our concern is the literary audience; the readers and the tactful approach to maintaining an audience through a posed grammatical language style intended for Believers and persons of all walks of life.

As a literary disclosure example, the word *"disinheritants"* an intended word usage by the author.

Our Maker, Defender, Redeemer, and Friend!

PROLOGUE SYNOPSIS

Black Theology tends to correlate with how Black people see God, the universe, the world and themselves from the pivotal vantage point of being the oppressed in a darkened society. Thus, the publication of this book entitled, "The Civil Rights of Black Theology," brings us to a new level of managing life by dissipating the everyday reflections of disparities, which have protruded through the economics of personal, social and spiritual injustices; to include personal venues which have consumed our mental being through trials and tribulations marinated with agony and pain. If cherished, the written text of this book shall spiritually alleviate the anguish faced by people of color, through the spiritual renewing of the brain folds; to include an uplift of one's spiritual subconscious state. Through the medium of this published instrument, we have been able to reveal a spiritual clarity by the critical formatting of its context.

Black Theology serves as the Eternal rock of defense for a people of color, due to the systemic denial of Black history in America; to include White America's despondency towards Civil Rights too. The momentum for life and living is predicated on Black Theology. Sunday's messages tend to draw and stimulate a massaging spiritual power to overcome the shadows of inequality and injustice with purpose. A theology which operates in both Believers and Unbelievers alike. Such theology intensifies with motivation to be courageous with endurance throughout the Black experience.

The Lord endorsed the Civil Rights Movement as an affirmation of His indebtedness towards a denied people which were posed *"disinheritants"* of their God-Indwelled rights, which are civil in likeness for all men. The Black Church was the chief cornerstone of the Civil Rights Movement; to include the teachings of her ethical theology of hope with tranquility. Her mission and sayings of that time, elevated a promissory theme of survival for a people of color. The mentioning of Civil Rights carries an unforgiving connation in the hearts of those who pose hate towards people of color. Even today, we are still being accused, despised, disapproved, refuted, refused, and rejected by the slated shadows of the Jim Crow theology. The draw of a Black Man or Women is not long enough to compete in a society which does not equate a fairness to all people, regardless.

God Himself invoked civil rights upon all humanity at creation. Civil and rights denoted human characteristics of equality upon mankind. Civil became the Divine essence of mortality; rights were intended as God-Given privileges; to include free choice of a righteous Will. We were created in His likeness, with equal rights appointed among all men from the beginning of creation. Even though, the snares and toils of life injustices were placed upon the being of our Souls, which tend to transfer into an economics of prolonged life-long personal, social and spiritual injustices. It has been said, each of us bear the burdens of personal injustices brought on by the Adamic nature of Sin and living.

The civil rights of mankind were Divinely formatted into the Garden of Eden scene with Adam and Eve as benefactors of those rights. The mentioned God-Given civil rights were violated by mankind through Sin. In the case of Adam and Eve, civil rights were marred by Sin. Afterwards, the civil rights of Abel were violated during the Cain and Abel episode. Thus, rights were recused in both cases, one by the preordained righteousness of God and the other by an unjust evilness of Cain, which was imposed against his brother. The case of Cain and Abel was devised by mortal evilness. Yet, both scenarios were perpetrated violations. One against God and the other against man towards himself. Thus, to this present, we are facing the hardships of life through the mediums of sickness, dying and death by way of everyday pain and agony. Now, we have been left with the chore of spiritually liberating and maintaining ourselves, until we make it across that chilly stream of Jordan. Applications of Black Theology has become a Divine mitigating process by which the text or story is lifted from the pages through an orator process, which liberates Black Souls through the muck and mire of the everyday scenario called living.

A Black Theology is the only platform of survival for a people of color. The strength of our Native soil is what keeps us day-to-day, without deliberations. It will have to be a theology of such which shall host a people for generations to come, even as we have struggled through the hisses of a hateful and unpredictable 2020. We have been a people who has defied the many odds through the worth of Black Theology. It keeps her people without their cognizance, even in the shadows of hate, injustice with poverty overlooking.

Black Theology seeks to explicate the Black Community's understanding of God's promises; to include the Lord's goals towards that which He is directing the world, while Black people in America are passing through dehumanizing life experiences. Yes, The Civil Rights of Black Theology has a definite propensity to liberate with a standing testimony. The strength of Black oration has a spiritual ability to shake trees and create confession to a dying Soul. The Ole *"Marster"* did not allow preaching on the plantation, because of a potential outburst and revolt within the slave community. Preaching was recanted and disallowed, due its liberating power. Mind me, there is epitome of our 21st Century preaching from the pulpit of Black Pulpiteers. A whooping tone which liberates the shackled Soul. Somebody stated, it was the Lord that kept Negroes sane. We must agree. The externals of life have mitigated to affect the internals of life; to include the mental physic of the conscious and subconscious. The state of our mental faculties dictates the vitals of our body organs and pulsations. As you read, self-liberate yourself. Find your way through by cherishing verses of this book, which best suit your being, livelihood and spirituality. This too shall alleviate the pains and sufferings which have been imbedded into the adrenaline of Black Folk. Dr. Michael Martin Luther King, Rosa Parks, John Lewis and Jesus the Christ, self-liberated and maintained themselves. It's strange, but true. We were born out of despair and then into despair, punctuated with hope. Let this mind be in you, which was also in Christ Jesus. Thereafter, shall consolation come forth, upon the Soul by way of your faithful prudence and God's Divine Wisdom.

PROLOGUE

This book has been written in poetic format to bring the reader into an atmosphere which creates a personal aspiration to become self-motivated with a stance of maintaining spiritual survival in spite of the present day situations surrounding their world of living. More or less, the textual style has been considered and categorized as empowerment to the Soul of each reader with much to be *"had and learned."* The text has a most permeating ability to draw one's thoughts into a quest with a higher dimension of thought processing. This book has been designed with a giftedness of seeing into the reader's perceptions of his or hers thought processes as they affect the mobility and motility of one's life. There has been a significant prophetic move of God to create a propensity through the worth of this book for readers to become energized for human survival in body, mind, Soul and Spirit. Make discovery of your premise and self-worth through the context of this book. As the reader, you will find words of unsuspected prophecy, spiritual motivation, spiritual empowerment, seasoned with a hint of humor, personal query, wisdom, senses of persuasion and even answers to life's questions.

We are His people, we His care.

INSPIRED INSPIRATIONS FOR BLACK LIVING

Life for 'people of color' has always gravitated towards the means of survival in the midst of darkened hope with dim realities. The depravities of life held us in shackles and fetters without a sense of being. We suffered the hardship of being shipped through darkened nights as crated freight, bound to an unknown landing; whence our days were still filled with the same darkness. Hopelessly, we sailed towards a dark and unknown tunnel of life. Our destiny was not mapped out of our own will, but by the intolerant Will of greed and Black economics from a White intent of personal satisfaction. In the midst of it all, the Lord genetically modified endurance to become strength by which we being examples of Hope, we became Hope.

We can hear the hymn writer saying, "Must I be carried to the skies on a flowery bed of ease, while others fought to win the prize and sailed through Bloody Seas." As a hymn writer, he was making mental emulations of the Swing Low, Sweet Chariot, coming for to carry us home, being only for those who paid the price; those who fought, those who suffered the Bloody Seas of chains, shackles and fetters.

Those who survived the dark tempest of a journey; landed only to meet White men at what was called the *"auction blocks"* of slave trade; to be introduced for the first time to fields of white cotton on plantations. These are they who were corralled like livestock for the *"marster's"* good pleasures, while bearing their burdens in the heat of the day.

It's a most mystical mirage, which has hampered the lives of Black Folk from the beginning of times even unto this present day. It took every fiber, needle, and thread to achieve victories in the midst of defeats; to gargle with one's own pee to heal the aliments of a sore throat. Where our ancestors used a forked tree branch to find unground well-water.

I Believe deep down, we mimicked the modern day stethoscope into existence through the imagination of our ancestors. Yet, we must not be naïve to the fact of God's Amazing Grace which came with us from a far way land to an unseen new world, which a culture and language change was incited upon us; to include our names being changed as a medium to deprive thoughts from our minds of our Native names in the Mother Land. Without consent, we bore the *"marster's"* name, even until now.

The same rugged cross Jesus endured has to be the same rugged cross which we must endure and even the more, because of the facing realities. His cross, based upon our ancestor's beliefs was rugged for a rugged people to come. Endurance and holding one's head up in spite of difficulties, creates a brighter day, whereas darkness must cooperate.

In spite of my people aggrieved deportation from portals of what they knew as the *"Mother Land,"* where all hardships came in anguish, but still their Souls felt Heavenly bound. In the midst of a swallowing sea, they saw darkness, but felt

Heavenly bound. They prepared us to be a people which must endure with a sustaining ability to overcome the shadows of darkness in a tilted world. In midst of agony, we were left with an inheritance of believing in the same God, to whom they prayed; the One to subdue hardships of uncertainties.

Even as Paul and Silas, chained, shackled and jailed...We too must pray, while we "sang," "Must Jesus Bear the Cross Alone," "Father, I Stretch my Hands to Thee," along with "Dark the Night, Cold the Ground," African American lives must be driven with purpose through a victorious mainstay of the mind, without being condemn and victimized. The purpose of this book is to give insight into the *"Black Experience,"* which has been the most construed and misinterpret by design, within our society. The African American population in America has been systematically socialized through the mental state of one's inability to think greatness; to the point which our younger generation has no knowledgeable concept of the ongoing Black struggle.

Throughout generations the academic mindset of Black America has been tempered and tampered by imposed restrictive learning of all kinds. Yet, the Lord left us with what it takes to be all one can be, without mind altering stigmas, which have been passed down for four hundred years. Apostle Paul told Timothy to stir up the gift which is within thee. Paul knew the genealogy of Timothy; he knew the unfeigned Faith, which was in Timothy. Likewise, African Americans have a proven unfeigned Faith dwelling within.

Achievement and greatness with power come from within the mind, as we translate the greatness of minds to minds. Conclusively, Black Theology warrants the stance of being spiritual endowed with power as of no other; to include an unction defined by Black endurance. Black Theology serves as an intuitive medium by which the denied can become empowered to overcome.

The Montgomery Bus Boycott portraits the evidence of a people with a theological mindset of maneuvering themselves through the onslaught of human injustices. A people of color with a defined skillset to exert themselves mentally and physically and spiritually through theological restructuring of the brain folds; to accomplish the unheard in a White society. This book has lent a passionate literary intent for the sake of body, mind, and spiritual empowerment; to include restoration of lost Souls. There are prophetic words platted with Wisdom within the text. A Divine imparted Word shall empower a Spiritual mainstay for those seeking a peace of mind in this most uncertain age.

This published book can never replace the Holy Scriptures, but will serve for personal meditations of comfort, teaching, counseling, preaching, while gravitating the mind towards a positive medium of translating thoughts; to decrease the intimidations of defeat, while living in this most vile world.

Photo by Canva.com

Photo by Canva.com

PROVERBIAL ESSENTIALS FOR BLACK LIVING 1

1. Sooner than later, the Lord shall rescind the evilness of the once imposed pandemic, which plagued the lives of His people. Sooner than later, we will once again, enter into His gates with Thanksgiving and enter into His courts with praises to get our shout on. Sooner than later, His promised decree shall go forth defeating the odds while declaring...upon this rock, I have built My Church and the gates of Hell shall not prevail against her, nor her people.

2. Right and righteousness have become an oversight in the New Normal. It behooves God's people to find their own situation room...where burdens, concerns and cares can be laid before the Lord in prayer, that there be no political oversight. Father God, shepherd us that you may lead, that we may follow and that Goodness and Mercy shall cover our backs...so be it, even the more Lord.

3. At the allowance of the Almighty God, and without any discretions, death is thereby summoned with its sting to disrobe us all of what we here possess. Be reminded, Momma would say, be ready, when He comes. Father God, on another day... we Thank You for bringing us up and out of yester night's sleep as we slept in the shadows of death. Now, guide us through this day as summer sails, even the more, right now.

4. I *"clare fore"* God, the best part of waking up is coffee in your cup and a mind stayed on Jesus, that our cup may *"run*

neth" over. Father God in Heaven, we, Thank You for the Blessings of Life, as we have slumbered and slept through night's darkness. Father, make good our living this day, that You may be Glorified through Christ Jesus, our Lord, even the more...

5. We are living in the midst of an indifferent people, copied and pasted onto an indifferent world which has trouble leaning on every side, while death is rampaging to destroy. It behooves you to make sure the door posts of your Soul have been painted by the Blood of Jesus.

6. As we venture into a New Year, let's avoid getting *"stuck on stupid."* That is...when God's perfect purpose and Will for us seems to be a hinderance to our personal agendas; that's when we hotwire or short circuit His Will to become our own will. Remember, His way is a lamp unto our feet and a light unto our path. He does not have to get to the end to know the end. He is the end. Life is better His way or no way.

7. At all cost, let's avoid getting *"stuck on stupid."* One day, a student left campus and walked to the nearest traffic light; carjacked a lady's car. The lady jumped out. While dialing 911, the student got behind the steering wheel; to his stupid surprise, the car was a stick shift. While still behind the steering wheel and *"stuck on stupid,"* the student could not make the car go. Nevertheless, the cops arrived with a brand new pair of stainless steel bracelets.

8. Again, as Momma would say, every dog got his day.

9. Don't commit the crime, unless you can pay the time.

10. Most of all, never ever get "*stuck on stupid.*"

11. Learn to filter your thoughts to avoid impulsive decisions.

12. Never invest in mess; go for success.

13. She said, that she was tired of being pushed around by everybody. Yes, I can imagine, it being one time too many after she boarded the bus. Then and then only, did the Lord look beyond the portals of Glory and saw us, to send His People a "*Rosa Parks,*" to leave a seat for us in the front of the bus.

14. Just about daybreak, this Father backed his car out of the driveway and headed off to work. OOPS! He remembered something back at home. Quickly, he returned back; he drove into the driveway; ran in the front door, and there...his baby son was brushing his dog's teeth with his Daddy's toothbrush. His father said, son? How long have you been doing this? The little boy said, forever. Take heed, lest the Lord may run in your front door, when you least expect.

15. Momma said, be ready when He comes.

16. This young church lady left town one morning and traveled to another city for visitation with a hospitalized Elder from her church. Upon her arrival to the visiting city, she found the hospital and immediately went to his room. After getting in the

room, the Elder was asleep, but she sat quietly waiting for him to awakened. While she sat quietly, she snacked on the peanuts from his tray table. Finally, the Old Elder awaken. Immediately, she began to apologetically apologize for consuming all of his peanuts from the tray table. The Old Elder said, "*Baby that's alright, I done sucked all the chocolate off them anyway.*"

17. Be careful about eating peanuts from other folk peanut dish.

18. It has been said, time tells the whole story of our lives. It tells who we are...what we have done, who we have been hanging with...tells our learning and bringing up, tells who we have been with the most, tells who we love the most and who shall be in our hearts, when the Lord shall call us from labor to reward. It is declared before God to be the truth.

19. A visiting elderly Pentecostal preacher from the foothills of the Appalachian Mountains approached the podium to bring the morning camp meeting message. He told the waiting congregation that it's a bad thing when you stop growing up and start growing out, because your arms and belt keep getting shorter at the same time.

20. Take heed lest you faint. All of Satan's gifts come from below and beneath; right straight out of the pits of Hell.

21. All good and perfect gifts come from above; straight from Heaven.

22. If you have to think about it long, it's wrong.

23. Yet, God's Gifts are perfect and come directly from above and not from beneath.

24. If Heaven did not give it to you, you really don't want it; nor the penalty thereof.

25. Black preaching is a powerful language, interpreted through the Gospel presentation in the context of Black miseries and Godly Hope for a people of color.

26. Black preaching has a prophetic voice in life's wilderness, crying out from within the Soul of hurt and pain.

27. Black preaching does all to reclaim her heritage while preserving her people.

28. Lord, we pray, you will execute your righteous judgement upon that which has come against your people. Lord you have assured us, no weapon formed or forged against us shall prosper.

29. "This is not the end, but the end of the beginning." (Winston Churchill).

30. The ongoing effects of the New Normal has cast a dim shadow of the Old Jim Crow into the lives of God's People with no respect to Black nor White; no respect to Color nor Creed to a galling gimp of lives without matter.

31. It was overheard: This man told his wife that his boss invited him to attend an all weekend fishing expedition with the company. The man said to his wife, baby, this might lead me to a promotion. Fix me up a small tote bag with my overnight stuff in it. The man returned home late Sunday evening. His wife asked, how was the fishing trip? The husband said, baby it was fine, but you forgot to put my pajamas in the tote bag. The wife replied, did you check your tackle box? That's where I put the pajamas.

32. Thought he was calling his girlfriend, but by accident, this man called home. His wife answered instead of his girlfriend. At unawares, quietly, he told his wife instead of his girlfriend, that he was taking his wife Out-of-town for the weekend. See, God don't like ugly.

33. Cheating on the wife is not cordial in the sight of the Lord.

34. The God-Given virtual of a woman is marred as she cheats on her husband.

35. Your Sin will find you out through a boomerang effect. Always, Sin identifies the Sinner of the Sin.

36. Be mindful: *"STAND YOUR GROUND,"* applies to whose ground you are standing and to whom the ground belongs.

37. WARNING: Driving while Black is like driving while DRUNK. It ain't a myth.

38. It's time for a change, give us what you owe us. (Unknown Singer)

39. Within the valley of the shadows of death, our Brother, George Floyd, cried out for his Mother through the timing tones of death, by uttering "*Momma*" in the languishing seconds of his life. His despised death broke the silence of all mankind throughout the world. Scripture reminds us of Jesus and His despised death too. He cried for His Mother by saying, Mother, "*behold thy son.*" Thus, the course of history was changed forever.

40. And seeing the multitudes, He went up into the mountains. We were that multitude. There, the Lord God provided for Himself, when he sent His only...Dr. Michael Martin Luther King Jr. as the Chosen One, to become a type of Christ for us; His People of Color and all humanity, as a Race of People.

41. Goodness and Mercy cannot not follow, if you are sitting on your bottom waiting on Goodness to come your way.

42. Jesus left the privilege and right of prayer for us to utilize. He said, man ought to always pray and faint not. The text suggest that in the midst of prayer, there is stance and stability.

43. For thirty-three years, Jesus lived through times and seasons of pending death.

44. We are living in turbulent times, where Evil wants to lurk its ugly face. Yet, Our God shall supply all our needs according to His Riches in Glory.

45. A few Sundays ago, a middle school student visited his classmate's church. The Spirit got real high; filled with dancing and shouting. The visiting student asked his classmate...Why are they dancing and hollering like *"that?"* The classmate re-plied, they've got the Holy Ghost. Come Monday morning, the classmate asked the visiting student, what did he think of his church? The visiting student bluntly said, *"Off the chain,"* but *"I don't want the Holy Ghost."*

46. Your funeral will be one appointment where you will not be late, because someone else will schedule your appointment and will bring you to your appointment.

47. Why does conflict have to be AMPLIFIED?

48. It's okay to disagree, but not be disagreeable.

49. You may have the greatest Faith. Yet, discreet reasoning must go with Faith.

50. It takes the Lord to exalt you, because man won't give you a chance.

51. The Blessings of God have a tendency to shun themselves from a liar.

52. Every soldier in God's Army possesses the same rank.

53. The woman with the issue of blood taught us how to think for ourselves.

54. The woman with the issue of blood taught us how to speak for ourselves to ourselves.

55. The woman with the issue of blood taught us how to press our way towards the prize.

56. The deacon was sound asleep in the bed with his wife, until he turned over in the midst of a slumber and thought he was still in bed with his girlfriend, after coming home from a drunken stupor.

57. Guess what?

58. He ran out of his own house with clothes-in-hand, trying to get home before daylight.

59. The next sermon will be entitled: *"Leaving Home, Going Home."*

60. We never know what's going on in Heaven; we never know Heaven's full intent for our lives.

61. Our lives are filled with looking through tinted glass. We know in part and see in part.

62. God takes what looks like our demise to the very edge of pending death; then His Glory comes forth.

63. Yet, we are most ungrateful in our hearts at times, while the Lord Himself has been deemed worthy of the Glory for His Blessed Assurance.

64. Otherwise, our George Jefferson's swag sets into our mystic fame of a personified glory.

65. Sometimes, it's good to go a different direction from the situation by finding a personal prayer closet.

66. The Bible says, Hezekiah turned his head from the situation and glued his face to the wall in prayer. His wall became his situation room.

67. There are times when God breaks us down, to build us back up stronger and sturdy for His Glory and purpose.

68. Had You been there, my brother would have not died. If there be any blame, it's on us, not the Lord. Martha got life, dying, and death all mixed up.

69. There are times when we are lost in the shuffle too.

70. Nature lost her balance and went crazy during the dying hours of Jesus' death. He who held the world together was dying at the stake of wooden crucifix.

71. One day, I was that Sinner in despair; I sought God's Mercy Seat by prayer. Mercy heard and set me free.

72. We as people of God find ourselves living in a bubble with substandard lives, not to our greatest potential.

73. The best part of church folk lives are lived in crisis mode, because misery loves company.

74. Sometimes our minds are caught between a rock and a hard place which deflects our thinking.

75. Raised one way and taught another way.

76. Living another way and looking another way.

77. Listening another way and going another way; the wrong way.

78. Society has hindered our ability to take on the Mind of Christ. This era of digital technology and Social Media have dictated our thinking towards Spiritual Living. The Godly effects of the mind has dissipated from many Believers; to include our ability to Believe in the Living God. Christ is no longer the center of the thought process.

79. As we think, we actually change the physical nature of our brain.

80. We must protect our thought processes from toxins by utilizing mind control.

81. Our ears, eyes and the lust of the eyes can cause a lack of mind control.

82. Strong Faith in the Almighty God and yourself, stabilizes the thought processes; to include mind control.

83. The folds in our brain are constantly being redesigned by our daily thought processes.

84. What you process in the mind has tendencies to manifest itself over a period of time.

85. This is the logic to an idle mind being the Devil's workshop. He constantly attempts to rearrange the folds of the human brain for his gain and your loss.

86. Black preachers from generations past, were great men of God. They were known for locking up alone to receive a hearing from the Lord, while integrating their energies through meditation and prayer unto the Heavens for the sake of God's People and their personal expectations of the Lord.

87. A good pastor gravitates towards sound Wisdom and Judgement.

88. Whether good or bad, our thinking emits energy throughout God's Creation; to include Earth and Heaven.

89. The outcome is yours to receive. Your human feelings are always subject to place your outcome in danger.

90. The Lord has given each of us a dispensation of power. We have unreasonably limited ourselves as recipients of His bounty which has been prepared for those who Believe.

91. The brain folds of pigeons in the grocery store parking have been genetically altered through the thinking of their bird ancestors, who had a perceived trust of people as non-threatening. The brain folds of their offspring have been modified, not to immediately fly away when humans are near the parking lot, because generations before them were raised in the same parking lot.

92. The brain folds of the squirrels in the city park were altered by prior generations, to not fear humans. Their brain folds were rearranged and modified by their foreparents which were born and lived in the same city park.

93. These examples were given as means by which we must merit our Faith and trust towards the Lord through our daily thinking and mind altering energies.

94. The defense attorney skills of Jesus came out when He asked, His disciples, who do men, say I am? When the disciples gave forth an answer to His question of inquiry, He was able to interpret their answers as observations of their personal feelings and thoughts of Him. Their answers did not reflect how others perceived Him, but how they perceive Him.

95. The Lord will never ever serve as prosecuting attorney.

96.The Lord will never ever serve as persecutor either, because of His love for all humanity.

97. The Lord Himself, will serve as Judge on Judgement Day.

98. Now, I see where Jesus got His legal skills. Now, I know why, He is a lawyer in the courtroom. Surely, He is a most skillful defense attorney. God ask Adam a question. Adam, where art thou? The question was not asked, because God knew not where Adam had hidden. Our God had a legal motive for asking Adam for his hidden location. The question was asked by God for Adam's sake that he may know the graveness of his Sinful situation, which he faced. Then and then only, Adam saw himself and his condition. THE VERDICT: Guilty as charged.

99. These words were once echoed through a sounding voice of courage by a Black female. I am no longer accepting the things that I cannot change. I am changing the things, I cannot accept.

100. The method to our madness comes, when the Lord takes us to the very extremity that we may know Him as Lord, even the more.

101. Ole Man Job was taken to that very extremity of a total loss.

102. Just as I am, without one plea.

103. It is believed Garth Brooks stated, some of God's greatest gifts are unanswered prayers.

104. If Jesus got up out of the grave with all power, Satan does not have power which can take effect over God's Power.

105. We as a People of God must learn to utilize mind control. Ridding ourselves of toxins with purpose and intent of healing our minds.

106. Our thoughts grow whether good or bad through a re-structuring of the brain folds.

107. Unconfessed Sins destroys the mind over a period of time. Sin grows and manifest itself in a spiritual disease form.

108. Lord, I tried to do all I could, seems like nothing would do any good, but then I heard Jesus passing by. Then, I decided to give Him a try.

109. Daily on the job, I am persecuted, but not forsaken; cast down, but not destroyed.

110. Be Blessed going out and coming-in. Otherwise, if you take a Blessing out, you shall bring one in as the Lord has provided. Whenever we bring a Blessing in, we should take one back-out.

111. The above rule has good reason: When the Lord lay Blessings upon you, reciprocate with others.

112. Whatsoever is loosed on earth, shall be loosed in Heaven.

113. Whatever you take out will return back-in with you.

114. The forces of Evil are always pressing the way for good to be annulled. Where Sin abounds, Grace abounds much more.

115. As these little snotty nose Black boys were playing outdoors, I saw fun smiles on their faces while hearing one them saying to the others, my Daddy got a *"Chebrolay"* car.

116. Just the other day, a lady dialed the operator and asked, if I dial 9-1-1 and the line is busy, what should I do? The operator replied, hang-up and dial nine-eleven.

117. The year of 2020 caused the African American Worship Experience to be elevated to a higher dimension than ever before. Black worship has the purpose of bringing Blacks together after weeks of tying ends together. The year 2020 has made the Lord more REAL than ever before in the lives of worshippers throughout the history of our African American Churches. Singing, shouting and preaching will be to no end in the foreseeable years. A new dynamics will surface even the more for the Glory of Our God.

118. If needing time is your everyday issue with life, while you are on a roaring, running non-stop roller coaster, maybe you

need some *"ME"* time. Just make sure Jesus is invited and be-comes part of your *"ME"* time.

119. Just a little talk with Jesus, tell Him all about your troubles. He will hear your faintest cry and answer by and by.

120. A few Sundays ago, this little boy was sitting next to his Mother in church during the tithes and offerings period. The little boy looked up at his Mother with curiosity and said, Mother, why do you have to pay tithes, if Jesus paid it all? Don't let curiosity hinder you from giving your tithes and offer-ings as the Lord would have it.

121. Recently, this twenty year old female sailor gave her Grandma a telephone call by dialing the house phone number, because her Grandma's cellphone was not receiving calls. Grandma answered the house phone by saying, *"Hello."* Grandma it's me, Renita. The Granddaughter said, how are you doing? Grandma replied, I am frustrated with this new cellphone of mine. Nobody ever calls me on it. The Grand-daughter said, Grandma, tell me, what do you see on the front of your cellphone? Grandma replied, *"I see airplane mood."* The Granddaughter chuckled out with a crazy laugh.

122. The phone had a mood of a mode, while making Grandma be in a mood of being frustrated.

123. If your life is in *"Airplane Mood?"* Why not, *"Try Jesus."*

124. God gives imaginary gifts.

125. Only the Lord can teach greatness.

126. Black, White or indifferent, without a doubt, everybody you meet these days is fighting a battle or dealing with a struggle of some kind.

127. Life will make you mad, but make the best of a bad situation.

128. "Hold on, help is on the way." (Whitney Houston)

129. Worries and sufferings will not let us be, until we cross over the chilly Jordan.

130. On your behalf, no matter what you are going through, the sun will rise again tomorrow.

131. Life betides for a night, but joy cometh in the morning.

132. The angels "*keepeth*" watch over you all night long.

133. Time is a matter of Arithmetic.

134. "*If I could, but just touch the hem of His garment*" says, the woman with an issue.

135. Get glad; don't get "*MADD.*"

136. By glimpsing at the forecast of thing, we are living in a toxic world. As Momma use to say, "*monest*" mean men and

women, boys and girls.

137. Big Mommas have become extinct. Ain't no more Big Mommas to wipe away our tears.

138. All our *"Madeases"* have passed on into Eternity.

139. We are now on an ungodly meltdown of the unknown.

140. Contrary to God's standards, sexting and texting has become the New Normal.

141. Rich or poor, Black or White, life is what you make it to be for yourself.

142. I was in the convenient store the other day and this lady was spoiling her children with an early morning breakfast consisting of Thrust Buster sodas, gummy bears and candies. I told the lady, back-in-the-day, spoiling your child was getting them up out of bed to wash dishes, clean the toilet and raking the yard.

143. His being beaten, *"buked"* and scorned had taken toll on His body. His physical effects as a human being were destroyed to a diminishing disfiguration with a most despicable discoloration to the body. Blood was dripping from His hands; to include His feet. His lips and face were blotched and swollen by the blistering sun. Insects were biting; stripes on His chest; stripes on His stomach from the whipping plaits. His legs not broken, but

flesh protruded from within. Stray dogs began to crowd the scene with anticipation of whatever was left to come. Momma said, He never said, a mumbling word.

144. Dying and death ain't nothing to play with. The ground began to break open with a quake in reception to His body being received with a pleasure. Darkness cover the land. The sun eclipsed a horror scene. The moon took on a bloody hemorrhage. Life's short duration began causing Him to gasp for breath. Nature went crazy, while onlookers left the scene running for their safety.

145. Our Blessings still awake us in the wilderness. We have failed to Believe the intelligence of that same God, which surface in the wilderness as a cloud by day and a pillow of fire by night.

146. The Devil is a *"Mayhem"* with a maliciously injuring demeanor; seeking whomsoever he may devour. He comes yet to steal, kill and destroy with an objective of a damaging death.

147. If Grandma can do all things through a belt and a cup of coffee, we ought to be able to do all things through Jesus Christ.

148. Grandma said, you ain't too old to get a butt whipping either.

149. In the midst of times, man has given up his God-Given dominion over the earth, to Alexa, Androids, Apps, Satellites,

Software, Drones, Electronic Intelligence and even Siri. Be it known, these ungodly intelligences, now defines to whom we belong and to whom we must obey.

150. Santa Claus, go straight to the ghetto, *"cause"* I know what you will see. It was me. (James Brown)

151. He had tiny *"foots,"* and a tiny red nose. On Christmas Day He was born into the joys of this world. Easter Day, He arose.

152. As a people who God has brought up and out, we have shown Him very little preeminence by living a butt backwards life.

153. Abraham told Isaac, God will provide for Himself. Abraham knew God was the Giver of His only Son Isaac, while believing God for another Son after the sacrificing of Isaac. That's why in full Faith, Abraham stated to Isaac, God will provide for Himself.

154. Many times, the battle ain't ours; it's the Lord's.

155. A legitimate attempt of drawing to God must be exemplified before the Lord draws nigh to you.

156. While sitting in the airport terminal next to this elderly lady, the intercom announcer came on with preflight announcements: *"Keep a close watch on your bags. Do not accept items*

belonging to others. Report suspicious persons. All bags are subject to search. Thank you and have a good flight." Afterwards, the old lady said, *"they scare you half to death and then they tell you have a good day."*

157. Protect your hedges from Satan, because hedges sift out the evilness of Satan. Satan said to the Lord, you have a hedge around Job and I can't get to him. According to Book of Job, he looks for the hedges around you, around your house, and around all which you possess.

158. As his Mother was dying, she said, son, I will meet you at the exchange counter, where I will turn in my cross for a crown. Thought to be stated by the Reverend Al Sharpton.

159. Ain't no other way to victory, except by way of the valley experience.

160. An elderly old lady walked into the hardware store and shouted with complete anguish, *"my toilet is broken and I can't get up."*

161. Are there days when you feel like your toilet is broken and you can't get up?

162. The Black church as we once knew her, has lost her savory. She was the cradle of the Civil Rights Movement. At that day and time, nothing defeated her fervency.

163. The Black Church, as we knew her...has lost resilience. Her pulpit has become powerless.

164. Our pews are partially filled; even then with no power in the pews. We come, but to get our shout on, but nothing to live on the rest of the week.

165. Powerful Black preaching always remains relevant for living and sustainability of "*Black Lives*," which do matter.

166. Never assume that loud is strong and quite is weak. Wisdom is having a lots to say, but hardly saying it. May the quite be, "*strong.*"

167. This lady told her son that he could get a good wife out of the church. Yet, after six months, the son realized that he was in the wrong church.

168. This young man walked up to his Reverend and said, pastor I am getting ready to become a parent, but I don't know, if I am the Father.

169. The Old Deacon Mizz whispered in the pastor's ear and said, I "*clare fore God*," the Lord knows who the Father is.....

170. This single parent Mom complained to the Lord in warm tears, that she did not have any food and Christmas toys for her children. She cried, until there were no more tears. Finally, she came to herself by the power of the Holy Spirit. Suddenly, she cried out Lord, I thank you for what I do have.

171. Always thank God for the leftovers.

172. Ain't no shame in my game.

173. Ask and it shall be given. Many of us recuse ourselves from asking, because of self-pride.

174. Use the Lord's prescription for profitable living.

175. It is believed that Elizabeth Taylor told her husbands the same thing which Black preachers tell the waiting congregation on a Sunday morning. "*I am not going to hold you long.*"

176. One preacher said, some of us will miss Heaven by eighteen inches; the distance from the top of the head to the center of the heart.

177. The head tends to draw us from the Lord by the struggles of the mind, while the heart tends to draw to the Lord.

178. In my coming up days, if you didn't tell the truth about something, the old folk with a plaited switch in their hand would call you a "*BOLD FACE LIE.*" They didn't call you a liar, but in their eyesight, you actually became the lie, itself.

179. Do you have the George Jefferson mentality and swag?

180. The Prodigal Son left a perfect world and went into an imperfect world filled with grief and sorrow. Just to let you know, the other side has growing brown grass called wheat

seed.

181. Serious business issues came into play after the chicken and the pig became partners while opening a new restaurant. The dilemma arose with the ham and egg sandwich being placed on the menu. Well, they forgot their commitment to each other as partners. When it came to eggs, the pig wanted the chicken to lay all the eggs for free. Yet, when it came to the ham, the pig had issues with giving his life for the chicken to make the ham sandwiches.

182. If you ever go in business, go in business with yourself.

183. Know before you go. Think before you do.

184. If mankind collaborated an initiative to give more than receive, there would be no lacks or injustices in society.

185. What's so amazing about Goodness and Mercy is that they will follow you, as long as you follow the Lord.

186. This poor little boy at school stated, his Mom wants him to act crazy at school, so she could keep getting her check every month. This will become an unwanted repercussion upon this child's life. You will become what you are dramatizing.

187. "*Lookout Elizabeth, here I come.*" Ask Fred Sanford of his demise.

188. Learning some sense might be a little too late.

189. Old folk would say, we will understand it, by and by.

190. Back-in-the-day, parents raised children hands-on. Now, parents rear children. Otherwise, parents walk behind the rear of their children; instead of leading, showing and teaching children the way.

191. Momma would say, *"make-do wit whatcha got."*

192. Momma use to say, a lie won't stand by itself.

193. Momma would say, come here boy, so I can pound some sense in your head.

194. Years ago, a Grandmother verbally abused her Grandson by calling him a fool all of his young life. As a teenager, he believed that he was a fool with no real comprehension of the word.

195. In poverty as a child, he drank black pepper and salt water to fill his stomach from hunger. Now, he is a physician serving others.

196. Take one step and the Lord will take two steps, perhaps three.

197. Little acts of kindness towards others make a **BIG, BIG,** difference in the eyes of the Lord.

198. He says, I will remember your kindness in the times of your troubles.

199. This era of digital technology proves with evidence, the rapture of the church soon to come; then the gruesome tribulation.

200. The evening train may be too late; ain't no back, back, train get your load.

201. This teacher said to him that he was from a poor family. Also, she stole his breath out of him by saying, you are from a dumb family and school will be hard for you to learn. During this little Black boy's second grade year, he empowered his mind to make a difference, because of what his teacher told him. Now, he is a medical doctor serving others.

202. Folk will steal the breath out of your Soul at the most unwarranted moment.

203. This member came to her pastor after church and said, pastor I gave samples of my DNA for my family's genealogy tree. The results revealed that I am going to Heaven.

204. WARNING: Jesus gave shed blood, not DNA.

205. These bodies of ours are in a fallen state; leaking like a leaning tower.

206. You can come to God smelling like pig; the prodigal *"smelt"* like pig, but went back home to his Father.

207. Do you want to go back to the Father too?

208. We are more than Blessed. Have you been to the funeral of the little twin boys? One of the twins laid deceased in the casket; the other twin alive and dressed in the same clothing outfit as his brother, who laid in the casket.

209. Be careful when sharing your testimony of God's Goodness; both Black and White folk will hate on you.

210. The salt box says, when it rains, it pours.

211. No rest for the weary. Is that you?

212. Granny use to fuss and say, he did a *"piss poor"* job.

213. Always, no matter what, do a good job as unto the Lord.

214. After Sunday Service, an old country deacon walked up to the preacher and said, preacher, the ointment *"shun nough"* was high up in here today.

215. Two ambulances were summoned to a funeral in progress; one ambulance for a pregnant woman and the other for a man suffering a heart attack.

216. So what's your beef?

217. The state of repose before the presence of Lord is the most mitigating venue by which we may find solace in Him.

218. The Lord ain't hard of hearing. Every now and then, say, I love you.

219. There are times when you don't have to pray, because the Lord already knows what you want; I will give you the desires of your heart.

220. This pastor was walking with a member through his yard about early dark and he accidently stepped on the blade of a garden hoe. The hoe handle painfully slap him right in the face. The preacher shouted, Damn You! To the garden hoe, he exclaimed. His testimony has not been the same since.

221. After Sunday Service, the preacher came by for dinner at the house of a member. After finishing his first plate of food, he asked for another plate. This little 6 year old boy was sitting at the table shouted, yeah! Momma already said, " *You eat like a pig anyway.* "

222. This Mother told her little boy to tell the insurance man, she was not home, when he knocked on the door. Well, the little boy answered the door, when the insurance man knocked. The little boy told the insurance man, Mister insurance man, my Momma told me to tell you, she ain't home.

223. Lies really don't hold much water. Already tried and proven.

224. There is a leak in every lie somewhere.

225. A liar will not tarry in His sight.

226. One simply low-down lie will get somebody killed.

227. This little boy never could not properly pronounce his own name. His name was Herman Lee. People would ask him, what's your name son? He would always say, "*Thurman Lee.*"

228. One elderly church member stated, she would not be coming to the abbreviated Summer Sunday Services, because by the time she get up, brush her teeth, shower, dress, fix her hair, put on make-up and take her pills, the one hour summer services would be over.

229. An elderly Black gentleman had a stent placed into his heart. After the surgery, he asked the doctor, if he got all the broken pieces out of his heart. The doctor replied, I did not see any broke pieces. The old man replied, doctor my wife separated from me over forty years ago and my heart, still hurts.

230. Why? As a little boy in the Sunday morning church service, my head kept turning backward looking for Charles to walk into the church building. Why? The deacons always sung this hymn, "*Hey Charles to Keep, A God to Glorify.*"

231. Holy Matrimony must be sanctioned by the Lord; not by emotions of invisible love.

232. Love does not pay a stack of bills; only a sound marriage pay bills.

233. Uncle said, it's cheaper to keep her.

234. Uncle said, the only way he was able stay married to the same woman sixty-five years, he kept two jobs at all times.

235. The deacon's wife said, once he retired, he stayed around the church more than he did at home.

236. It's good to be an old man, but not an old fool.

237. The deacon's wife said, she would have to call the church to find her husband, because her husband *"don't"* know where home is...

238. The deacon looked down over his glasses at me with a blank face. I understood...

239. This man supposedly of the cloth, robed in wolf clothing, came up to this woman and said, let's go and get it on. She told him, that he was too short. The man made a rebuttal and replied, laying down, we are the same length. Then the woman said, what's done in the dark shall come to the light. The man made the second rebuttal and replied, let's keep the lights on. The woman recused herself of his awkward and ungodly fool

ishness.

240. My Daddy said, the children would sit around kitchen floor wall watching the preacher eat up all the good chicken. As children, they were left with the chicken *"foots."*

241. According to biblical standards for Black Folk, the chicken is the most sacrificed bird, because of the Black preacher.

242. It is believed that Sam Cooke said, as long as you stay in the fold, you don't have to worry about God's call from labor to reward.

243. This preacher was preaching against the Evils of drinking. He said, all the beer, wine, whiskey and alcohol ought to be thrown in the ocean. Right at the end of the service, he ask an Old Saint of a Sister to lead the congregation into a closing song before the benediction. The Old Sister started singing, take me to the water, take me to the water, take me to the water, and baptize me now.

244. On my way to GloryLand, but ain't made it there yet...

245. Just maybe, you need a bunny rabbit battery, so you can keep going and going for Jesus.

246. Aren't you glad you have Jesus? Don't you wished everybody did?

247. He is acquainted with all our griefs and sorrows; He

knows our faintest cry.

248. It has been a long, long, time coming.

249. God did not allow the rain to come, until after the last nail was nailed. Ask Noah.

250. The year 2020 most bitter sweet, but GOD...

251. America knows the worth of her people of color.

252. In the arena of Blackness, there has been a backdrop of undue injustices.

253. Somebody said, if I had strength in my pinky, I would move hate.

254. Suggestive to a SUPERNATURAL move of harassing hate.

255. The Lord is acquainted with the ruggedness of the cross borne by His People of Color.

256. God's people are tasked with building bridges, not walls of dissent.

257. Back in the day, being a Colored...you were labeled out of place. You had no place, except the church, provided she was not burned to the ground. Yet, the White Man words... *"Boy, you had better stay in your place."*

258. Daddy said, do what you think they want you to do.

259. Daddy said, say what you think they want you to say.

260. Daddy said, be what you think they want you to be, so you can make-do.

261. In spite of: The Lord has brought us from the Outhouse to the White House.

262. Black Democracy for all mankind, regardless of the hue.

263. Black Women, dream with ambition and conviction. (Kamala Harris)

264. Black Women, wear your White pearls as the Lord exalts His Women with Heavenly Honor.

265. In spite of the odds, you are *"Highly Favored of the Lord."*

266. Defeat despair. (Joe Biden)

267. Spread the Faith. (Joe Biden)

268. Find the way and follow it.

269. Jesus said, I am the Way.

270. Always, make good of your living.

271. Speak to yourself.

272. Hello self.

273. Good morning self.

274. I am Blessed self.

275. What a wonderful day, self.

276. Behave self. Don't let your ugly come-out.

277. You look terrific self.

278. Self, I speak over you now, in the Name of Jesus.

279. I can do all things through Him, and self.

280. Cooperate and Situate; many hands make lite work.

281. God made man differently from all other living creatures which were made.

282. God made man with a heart which allies to both the brain and Soul.

283. Sometimes, we can see the Hand of God working. Yet, not knowing what He is doing.

284. Sometimes, we can't trace His hand, but we must trust His Heart.

285. He has a Heart being driven by His love.

286. Once the heart, brain and Soul becomes aligned together in allegiance towards each other, Salvation culminates; bringing forth Eternal life unto the beholder.

287. "*His Blood be on us,*" their spokesman shouted. "*On us and on our children.*"

288. Better be careful what you say; be reminded a Holocaust of suffering, dying and death came.

289. Sometimes, being transparent on social media is not to your best benefit.

290. It's very offensive for children to say, WHAT to an adult.

291. Perhaps, the Lord has reserved you for such day.

292. Reach out and touch a hand; you just might be saving a weary Soul.

293. Reach out and touch a hand; make a friend, if you can. (Staple Singers)

294. As a People of God, we have been sedated by the influence of Evil, and the sting of Satan's demise.

295. The Lord gave us a plumb line by which all humanity must govern itself into healing with wholeness.

296. Finally brethren, whatsoever is true, honest, just, pure, lovely, and of good report, must be thought upon. Contrary to His law, we have navigated ourselves with relish to the untrue, the dishonest, the unjust, the impure, the unlovely and that of a bad report.

297. Society without God is destined to be doomed.

298. Lots of times we crap on ourselves. Then want the Lord to come and clean up the mess, instead of asking him to clean us up.

299. The little boy asked, how old are you, fifty-seven? My reply, Yes. His response, that's old. I replied, wait until you get fifty-seven years old.

300. After mentioning the name Santa Claus, this fourteen year old boy shouted, there ain't no Sandy Claus. "*I stayed up all night long and he didn't come.*" A rebuttal of a reply came back and said, that's why he didn't come.

301. The stain of Sin has saturating power and weighty weight.

302. Black Folk are undeserving one towards another, due to an underlining lack of genuine love.

303. Sometimes, you may not know people for whom or what they are...

304. A strong Black woman can make something of a weak Black Man.

305. Again, as paraphrased: It's been too hard living, but I am afraid to die, cause I don't know what's up yonder, beyond the sky.

306. At the point of a dying hour, one always think of what should have been done and what was not done.

307. The question has been asked, why do we suffer the suffering before a change comes?

308. The same ole struggles through a systemic underlining called, radical racism of a people.

309. A pot of good cooked Collars and Ham Hocks will feed your belly right up to the Soul.

310. Now, you know the definition of Soul Food.

311. Time always shows Mercy of some kind.

312. Ole Man Wisdom will show the way, if asked.

313. In the "*Hood*," we don't have "*mouses*," we have Toms and Jerry's.

314. Fear and ignorance will bring you down.

315. Surrender to God, what comes before your mind.

316. We must embellish our being into the Wonders of a Mighty God.

317. The Lord sets before us open doors, which we may see within; that we may enter therein.

318. Remember, your greatness came on the back of somebody else, even Big Mamma's prayers.

319. She was bent over and body bound in prayer for you.

320. You and I looked in the mirror to see ourselves, but twins look at each other to mirror themselves.

321. Avoid talking so much smack.

322. Avoid getting too BIG too quick.

323. Is your heart three sizes too small?

324. No wonder.

325. Some of us have risen to the top, but still can't see the sun.

326. Likewise, some of have risen to the top, but still can't see the Son.

327. Our God is far off, yet near.

328. Too wise to make a mistake; too just to do wrong.

329. The only differences in women are their ways.

330. Especially, when you intended to cuss the Hell out of somebody, the Lord, HELD you-on.

331. BEWARE: To openly joke about someone to their face is an underlining revolt of scurry.

332. A woman should robe herself in Grace, not skinny jeans.

333. As the old preacher from back-in-the-day would say, ain't no need in a Man or Woman whoring around.

334. Grace flows to the beholders and seekers of Grace.

335. Favor is sought after by the one desiring it the most.

336. If you find yourself going Northbound and Southbound at the same time, there are issues.

337. It is okay to remember back, but don't look back or you might "*stayback*."

338. To remember back and not look back, leads to a better future.

339. When a Believer messes up, the same Believer ought to straighten-up.

340. Are you the man in the mirror?

341. Are you the woman in the mirror?

342. Who and what do you see?

343. Is the real you in the mirror?

344. There ain't nobody else to blame.

345. If you want to live in HIM, you must confess HIM.

346. Some people not only turn you off, but away.

347. When people and situations come together, differences are forgotten.

348. All of us have found ourselves at one time or another, stuck between burdens and Blessings.

349. A fortunate man knows and can glimpse his destiny ahead of time.

350. "It's been too hard living, but I am afraid to die, *"cause"*I don't know what's up there, beyond the sky." (Sam Cooke)

351. If you give up on life, life will give up on you.

352. Momma done *"sang"*too long, "Burdens Down, Lord...Burdens Down" for you to go around stressing, while looking for a burden to pick up.

353. A constant Obedience, Praise, and Reverence always exerts with power, the Lord's Favor upon your life.

354. Obedience in pleasing Him through our everyday living.

355. Praise in pleasing Him through a constant mid-low voice of praise all day long.

356. Reverence in pleasing Him through a constant awareness of His presence all day long.

357. The Saints grunted their praise and reverence unto Him, due to unwarranted restraints.

358. The Old Saints discovered an inarticulate means of being heard by the Lord. Why can't we?

359. This is of our reasonable service unto the Lord, God Himself.

360. Always, make discovery of the meaning and purpose of

your suffering.

361. It's most ungratifying when somebody tells me, I can't.

362. God don't like ugly. Ugly cannot be erased, but forgiven.

363. Conclusively, there is a color difference in the matter of lives.

364. The old normal said, it was a misdemeanor, felony or worst for a person of color to wear a mask into a bank; the New Normal dictates and mandates a mask to be worn into the bank.

365. We are living in the days of Evil thereof; willful Sin is being cost calculated.

366. Concurrence says, our society has been plagued with a scale of Evil.

367. The strove for perfection can only be found on the other side of the Jordan River.

368. We must too press our way.

369. We see so much, but we do so little.

370. Never surrender to what seems like a failure.

371. We come prostrate before you like the woman with the issue of blood.

372. "*Clare fore God*," the Lord will see you through, anyhow and somehow.

373. What you don't want to happen, will happen. Ask Ole Man, Job.

374. What you desire to happen, struggles to happen. Ask Apostle Paul.

375. Ask yourself, who do men say, I am?

376. A stout heart will not tarry before God.

377. The tongue is deadly and unruly. Once you *"lite"* the match with your tongue, it can't be unlit.

378. Man's *"knowings"* and man's *"doings"* outrun each other.

379. The human senses do not deceive, but human judgement and human *"misjudgement"* deceives.

380. Guard your ears and eyes, without feeling overruled.

381. You must define yourself from deep within.

382. After immigrating to America, he noticed a narrow spectrum towards humanity, which is called racism.

383. Since the beginning of times, man has wanted to play the role of God Almighty.

384. The attempted coup started in the Garden at Eden; then the Cain regime. Now, to include the New Normal of 2020.

385. Don't try. A woman can never ever be figured-out.

386. There will be times in life, when it seems as if everything and everybody has conspired against you.

387. Being Black in America doesn't always make you feel safe.

388. Man must have Faith in human nature.

389. Man must have Faith in the nature of humanity.

390. It's required of our Soul, that adequate and quality time be set aside to rest our Spirit.

391. We live in a broken world, propped by Calvary's Cross.

392. Build at least ten minutes of do nothing time into each day for mediating and silent prayer.

393. Maintain an attitude of gratitude. Speak with gratitude and thanksgiving to yourself and others all day long; abundance will come your way.

394. Avoid drinking coffee with the Devil. He just might become your coffee mate.

395. Avoid being too big for your britches. Mamma says, you ain't got a pot to pee-in and no window to throw it out.

396. There were times, Momma would grab you by the seat of your britches and whip that fanny.

397. Momma says, He's a Company Keeper in a midnight hour.

398. Greatness comes through intentional kindness and servanthood.

399. Kindness and servanthood brings abundance to the beholder.

400. Regardless of what will or will not happen, it will happen either way.

401. Master of the sea in my disparity. Aint He?

402. Lord, send us a Blanket of a Blessing.

403. Spot your door posts with the Blood and the Death Angel will Pass over.

404. He will pass over. Salvation is in the passing over, but there is a prerequisite to prepare.

405. Grace Intercedes, while Prayer "*Intercesses.*"

406. I can fix it! You can't fix nothing; you can only make a mess of fixing stuff on your own.

407. Sometimes as people of God, we must sleep the drunkenness of our stupor-off, before we can think soberly as the Lord would have us.

408. On an individual basis, we as a people of God at awareness and unawareness are subject to "*problemate* (Latin) "his or her own problems; only to become infectious to ourselves.

409. If you ever get caught sleeping on the job, lift you head up; open your eyes and say, AMEN.

410. It seems as if getting married has become antiquated and obsolete.

411. Oh Lord, bottle my tears as my prayers being sent up...

412. I can feel and touch your presence within my Spirit, but the voice of my prayers are gone.

413. I am standing here, because you made a way...Oh Lord.

414. In 2021, we pray America retrieves from her fall with kneeling knees; then to her feet.

415. BELIEVE ME: Every time, Satan will attempt to prove you wrong.

416. BELIEVE ME: Every time, Satan will attempt to prove you as dirt.

417. If you ain't smart enough to know when Satan is around Or in your path, that's your Spiritual Shortcoming.

418. In Him, there is Grace beyond degree.

419. As often as ye do this, you do it in Remembrance of Me for the Remission of Sins.

420. The wafer for His Body; the grape juice for His Blood.

421. Looking up towards Heaven, He gave thanks.

422. Body and Blood of our Lord and *"Saviour"* Jesus Christ.

423. Take and eat ye all of it.

424. Take and drink ye all of it.

425. And they "sang" a hymn and marched to the Mount of Olives.

426. The White Linen on the Communion Table represents His Grave clothing.

427. The White Linen over the Communion Tray represents the cloth about His face.

428. The White gloves worn by the officiator and deacons, represent the purity of hands by the Redemption of His Shed Blood.

429. The Black Communion suit worn by the officiator and deacons, represents His Death.

430. The White Communion attire worn by the deaconess and women of the waiting congregation represents the radiant lightness of His Resurrection.

431. The White head piece worn by the women, represents reverence with submission unto the Lord as the Risen "*Saviour.*"

432. Death began to stare Him in the face, while the grave waited in anticipation for Him.

433. Jesus was assassinated.

434. His Civil Rights of equity and equality for mankind stripped; to include His life.

435. From the earth to the cross; from the cross to the grave, humanity redeemed.

436. The moon dripped down in blood through a bleeding hemorrhage.

437. The earth shook and staggered like a natural drunken man.

438. The story of creation and humanity culminated to a complete rearrangement of the earth.

439. Time found zones; destiny found divinity; saved found Salvation and the dying found Life Eternal.

440. Nature lost her mind, because her Creator gave His life for a dying world.

441. Death surrounded the scene with depths of darkness and fright.

442. Dark the night; cold the ground on which they laid my Lord.

443. Yet, He lived to died, that we might die to live.

444. Behind His death and our living, we hold the following truths to be self-evident....

445. Hush, somebody calling my name.

446. He is "*A Wonder, yes He is...*"

447. He is "*A Rock in a Weary Land.*"

448. He is "*A Shelter in the Midst of a Storm.*"

449. He is "*A Lawyer in a Courtroom.*"

450. He is "*A Doctor in a Sickroom.*"

451. He is "*A Battleaxe in the Time of a Battle.*"

452. And can be a Mother for the Motherless while being a friend for the friendless.

453. My All-N-All from Everlasting to Everlasting.

454. He can be the Judge, Lawyer and Jury all at the same time.

455. He confers with Himself for our defense and pleas.

456. He knows all Soul's diseases.

457. His Glory, my story.

458. God has spoken; let the whole church say, Amen. (Andrae' Crouch)

459. And all God's People say, Amen.

The Prayer of St. Francis

Lord, make me an instrument of Thy Peace; Where there is hatred, let me sow love; Where there is doubt, Faith; Where is despair, hope; Where there is darkness, light; and where there is sadness, joy. O Divine Master, grant that I may not so much seek to be consoled, as to console; to be understood, as to understand; to be loved, as to love; for it is in giving that we receive, it is in pardoning that we are pardoned, and it is in dying that we are born to Eternal life.

St. Francis

PROVERBIAL ESSENTIALS FOR BLACK LIVING II

1. The old preacher says, always do what is right, even in the midst of adversities.

2. Substance abuse is being nitty with what God has provided.

3. Never get caught in your own dilemma.

4. The days of righteousness are far gone from mankind; do what makes you feel good is the New Normal for a lost and HELLBOUND society.

5. "It's your thang. *Do whatcha wanna do.*"

6. God had and has an intended plan with purpose for life; mankind has missed that plan with no purpose.

7. The old landmark has been erased with tarnish.

8. What's done on the front page of life, will be done on the back page too.

9. Tell that Sinner, time is winding-up. God's *"gonna"* move His hand.

10. This Son stood over his Mother's dying bed, while complaining about his Sister; the Mother, through the weakness of her voice said, Son, just you do right...

11. Revelation 3:8 says, God has your back when there is little strength.

12. Greatness comes through kindness and servanthood.

13. May the work you have done, speak for you.

14. Sometimes God's intent breaks us down to bring us back-up.

15. Every now and then, turn your head to the wall and cry-out a prayer unto the Lord.

16. Many of us are living below the established pedigree of life as prescribed by the Lord.

17. Most of the time, God assigns a holding pattern before His Blessings come through.

18. Don't be fooled by waiting for the promise.

19. In the midst of life, there is always a process of adjudication taking place.

20. Some people are so caught up in themselves, till they don't see nobody else, except themselves.

21. Sometimes caught up in self, will cause you to lose sight on the Lord.

22. Momma taught us to take the bad with the good.

23. Good dissipates bad...

24. Otherwise, deal with it. Job said, in all my appointed times, I am going to wait, till my change comes.

25. There are two dark shadows in the valley; death and yours.

26. Death is hard to explain.

27. Death has its own ample time.

28. There's a method to the madness. That's why Jesus stayed, until Lazarus died.

29. His ways are pass our "*understandings.*"

30. Maybe the last time, we walk together again.

31. Maybe the last time, we sing and shout together again.

32. Maybe the last time, I don't know...

33. Tomorrow, may not come on tomorrow.

34. Power in that Name.

35. Jesus is that Name.

36. Hush, somebody's calling my name.

37. He is a wonder in my Soul.

38. That's why my Soul says yes...Yes, Lord.

39. I got a *"feelin, everythang gonna be alright."*

40. Momma told me so; Jesus too.

41. Walking and talking with Jesus on my mind.

42. Bound for Mount Zion, if anybody makes it, surely, I will.

43. Don't you *"wanna"* go to that land, where I am bound?

44. Bad with the good is an appointed time for us to take up the slack with ugly situations.

45. Momma would say, come here boy, so I can learn you something. Actually, she was saying *"teach you something."*

46. Do your part and the Lord will do the rest.

47. Momma says, baby God knows.

48. Sometimes, the Lord gives us opportunity, that we may find our way.

49. We must hold our heads up higher than high in the midst

of our valley experiences.

50. Sitting on a lazy butt and praying won't do; Faith without works, won't do.

51. Do good by your money and your money will do good by you.

52. Ain't no hope in LOTTO.

53. The difference in a Caretaker and Caregiver: The Caretaker, takes care. The Caregiver, gives care.

54. The difference in Carry-Out and Take-Out: Carry-out is ready to eat food as you carry it out. Take-out is food made to order and taken home to eat.

55. If you have been thrown under the bus, just don't let the tire tracks run you over.

56. Never become anybody's Roadkill.

57. Our society has hijacked Christianity as a scapegoat for injustices towards people of color.

58. The WORD says, Fret not thyself, because Evil injustices. (Psalms 37)

59. It does not matter how high your corporate ladder ascends, your roots *"come"* from the HOOD.

60. The ruggedness of Black Theology brought us from the church house to the music halls, the silver screens of Hollywood and sports arenas; to include the CEO highchairs.

61. Black or White, there shall never be an intent or purpose to distract us from our intent or purpose to love one another, as Christ so loved us.

62. It has been tried and proven that people of color maneuver more successfully with endeavors, when being mentored or sponsored by persons of a different color.

63. It is agreed. America's culture and racial diversity creates a beneficial asset for all people of color.

64. No other country on the globe can compete with America's diversity. Structural racism has no place in America.

65. This family was driving into this little town, which had a huge cemetery on the side of the highway. While driving by the cemetery, this Father said to himself in an audible voice, I wonder how many people are buried out there in that cemetery. One of his little children shouted, Daddy, all of them.

66. An old man went to the doctor, while there, he ask the doctor, if he will he be able to make it another week or two.

67. Avoid the void in your mind; then substantially will gravitate into your spiritual being.

68. There is hope in our dreams. Dream on.

69. It's not that you don't want to, but it's that you don't want to take the time to...

70. Avoid letting your mind wander down into the valley; the valley is the aboding place of the Devil.

71. Sometimes, what you are looking for does not exist as expected.

72. There are steps to a victorious life; find them and climb them.

73. When an old widow woman walks out on her back porch and finds a man breaking into her shed, she shouts at him and he freezes with shakes and trembles. The cops comes and the man is still frozen with shakes and trembling. The cops ask the old widow, what in the world did you say to him? The old widow said, I shouted Acts 2:38. This would be thief cried out, no officer, she said, "*she had an ax and two thirty-eights.*"

74. This single parent Mom had seven sons. So one evening, before bed she got her sons together and told each one what he was to be in life. Finally, she got to the last son and said, John, you are going to be Momma's little preacher. So little John went off to bed and thought about the thing which was told him by his Mother. Finally, little John came back to his Mother's room in the middle of the night and awakened her up. Little John said, Momma, I don't want to be a preacher.

75. Believe it or not, evilness has been imposed upon man kind; we are left with mustering ourselves through by way of prayer and praises unto the Lord.

76. Old folk use to chew table food and then feed it from their mouths to the baby's mouth.

77. I can hear the old folk saying, "*the Lord been good by me.*"

78. It's your own fault, when you find fault in everybody and everything;

79. Be it known, our whole world is in a fault-fallen state.

80. Don't be so hard on yourself. Talk to the Lord, He understands your faintest cry.

81. Whatever it may be...Don't boast about it, just speak it into existence.

82. Either we are coming out of a storm or going into a storm. Perhaps, we are right in the midst of the storm.

83. A good husband can see farther than his wife and children, because his job is to look *"OVER"* the family. He looks over the present, then back through the past into the future.

84. Church folk are guilty of strangling the church, when it comes to tithes and offering.

85. Church folk are guilty of frustrating the pastoral leadership, which places limitations on the God's vision for the church. A frustrated pastoral leadership becomes dim sighted with no prospective vision for the local church, nor her people.

86. Church folk lack the wisdom of knowing a real man of God, who has a heart after God.

87. A real pastor must possess the Heart of God. I give pastors after My own heart says, the Lord.

88. A real pastor has a passion for the flock, when he smell like his sheep.

89. A real pastor has a passion for all humanity, without regards to the personal status of his ego.

90. Preachers are strange creatures to be reckon with in the likeness of mankind.

91. Preachers must adapt to being a friend only to themselves, due to suspicion and superstition; the inability to entrust personal biases and emotional concerns with others.

92. Pastor wives are withdrawn into the sea of loneliness, apart from this present world for a loss of mentorship and peers with a level of trusted integrity.

93. Preacher kids suffer an unmitigated endowment of non-negotiable respect as children of the preacher and his wife. So-

ciety's standards for living are thrown upon them as perfect people.

94. Every action mandates a reaction. Every reaction mandate an action back. Avoid living life with futility.

95. Always have a plan. Know what you are doing; know where you are going.

96. We are always trying to rediscover ourselves. For what reason?

97. Draw nigh to me and I will draw nigh to you. Who's doing the most drawing? You or the Lord?

98. Instead of being led by the Lord, some of us stand in need of being herded by the Lord for the sake of our own Salvation.

99. Some folk, the Lord can't lead. His has to herd them thru trials and tribulations; to get them where they need to be...

100. The path of righteousness is narrow. If more travel therein, the way widens.

101. Don't get your dandruff all raised up, because of crazy people.

102. When other folk hate befalls you, recycle and let it roll off your back.

103. Takers take; givers give; but takers must endow themselves to become givers, instead of being takers.

104. Every now and then, trust chance and give. Then give chance, a chance to give back to you.

105. If the Lord say-so, I will see you on tomorrow, if the creek don't rise.

106. All we can do is be a friend to this dying and unfriendly world.

107. The Lord Loves cheerful givers.

108. Should not it be "*teethbrush*," instead of toothbrush?

109. Avoid letting your flesh rare-up against others when good fortune comes upon them.

110. This little boy accidently sneezed on his school teacher. Immediately, he told his teacher the sneeze was a Blessing, not a sneeze.

111. This little boy told his Daddy that he was going to run away from home. His Daddy immediately said Son, you don't have to run; just walk away. The little boy made no attempt of running away from home. Tough love is a parent's best friend for showing a child the way.

112. Four little kids were playing kickball. A little White girl, a

little White boy and two Black boys. One of the little Black boys suddenly said, we are going switch and have a Black boy and a White girl team. What a crazy smile appeared on my face.

113. One day little Black boys and little White girls will be holding hands with...

114. Take stock in your children; reap the dividends later.

115. There are times in life, when we charge ourselves with a verdict of guilty.

116. Avoid letting Sin have its permissive way in your life; God forbid.

117. If we are caught embezzling SIN, the consequences can be most detrimental to the Soul.

118. People will hate on you, because of who and what you stand for...Jesus and His Righteousness.

119. Lord, give me an appointment to receive my anointing.

120. Our perception of greatness can mislead to downfalls.

121. Good or bad, the tongue is a most powerful weapon.

122. Wrong can never be right. Right has the stimulus to stand on its on merit.

123. Once obtained, the Holy Spirit promotes a quality balance to life.

124. Greatness comes from the bottom up; not the top down.

125. At the name of Jesus, burdens get lighter; the day get brighter.

126. Go for the aluminum and copper before the silver and gold.

127. Avoid accelerating ourselves pass our means.

128. Avoid keeping up with the Joneses.

129. Inside The Joneses' house is horror and terror.

130. On the other hand, The Joneses rather have what you got.

131. You had better hold on to what you got.

132. Life as we once knew it, has dissipated from the normal equation.

133. Our world has turned upside down; Grace and gravity keeps us from falling off the globe.

134. This world is reeling and rocking; man has outgrown himself to become a destructive creature.

135. Man has defunct his God-given humanity for the preexistent role of being a creature.

136. Man's destructive demeanor has become contrary towards God's Creation.

137. Gaining the world and losing your Soul is most deadly.

138. In uncertain times like these, lots of us can't pray straight, because we possess *"junk in the trunk."* Lay aside every Weight and Sin that so easily beset us; that we may pray straight.

139. New millennium parents must raise their children the same way as the old millennium parents once raise us. If not, consequences are most *"betrodden."*

140. *"Yes Ma'am." "No Ma'am." "Yes Sir." "No Sir." "Stay out of grown folks busy."* Bring me a switch. Come here boy! Stop lying boy! Don't talk back to me boy! Straighten your face up!

141. Momma in her reputable and most rebuttable demeanor would say, come here boy! So I can knock some sense in your head.

142. Some women will run a good man away.

143. Momma would say, a piece of a man is better than no man.

144. Some men take a good woman for granted.

145. Men, remember a woman is always two steps ahead of you.

146. Hate makes Haters. Haters and Hate bring on extenuating circumstances, which can set on fire the course of nature.

147. Our extremity is God's opportunity.

148. The Lord is amazing, just like His Grace.

149. The Old Folk had a saying. "*If you do right, right will follow.*"

150. Be not deceived for God is not mocked. Never play games with the Devil. He does not play fair.

151. Satan is like a devilish child; always wanting the final say-so.

152. Satan is like an old devilish kitchen fly.

153. The Devil is a shyster.

154. The Devil leads.

155. The Lord guides.

156. Everything you need is in the "*House of the Lord.*"

157. God's Goodness goes hand-in-hand with our Faithfulness.

158. Come on in the room, Lord.

159. All too often, Blacks and Whites, vote against each other by voting Color instead of the issue.

160. The culture of Black America has rapidly changed from Black survival to Black denial within her own people.

161. The culture of the Black Church has rapidly changed from the church, which Momma "sang" in the #2 Choir.

162. For generations even to now, people of color have settled for appeasements.

163. Black Folk were looked upon as property, not as human beings.

164. Mothers ended the lives of their children for the avoidance of brutality posed by slavery.

165. Many times, a mother separated her daughters and sons, while fleeing the reins of slavery.

166. She did all to protect her girls from rapes and molestations imposed upon them by "*slave masters.*"

167. We have come a long ways, but not far enough. Sometimes, we are called "*You People.*"

168. Ain't no difference than being called "*Coloreds.*"

169. People now days live like there ain't no right in *"Right-eousness."*

170. God loves you in spite of you.

171. I am so glad the Lord don't call me a *"Newby."*

172. I am so glad Salvation does not come with a probationary period.

173. People of color have been bought and sold for generations, even unto now.

174. Now days, we barter for favors, while denying the integrity our struggles.

175. People of color have been *"genocided"* with a weakness of despondency.

176. Our days, few and full of troubles.

177. You can't change who you are...you are who you are.

178. Thank you Lord for picking me up by the boot straps.

179. Waking up every morning is a fringe benefit with perks.

180. If a man die, shall he live again?

181. Jordan River, I am bound to cross; just one more river to

cross.

182. Never debase yourself. Your good Will is bigger than life's obstacles.

183. Avoid salt and peppering you dialect with vulgarity.

184. Solitude with the Lord is far better than rubies from the Far East.

185. Don't frustrate, liquidate frustrate.

186. Sometimes, you have to challenge the mind to behave.

187. The blood of our ancestors has a message for an undue society.

188. Unwarranted, inappropriate, because of excessive disproportionate profiling.

189. America will never-ever find consolation from her Sins towards Black America.

190. People of color live under the constant shadows of despair and disparity.

191. The Black Man's ballot by fraud, force or whatever.

192. By ballot splitting, fish dinners or whatever culminates a defeat to people of color.

193. The question was asked? "What shall be done with the Negro?"

194. It takes a Negro his whole life of struggles to get a good name for himself.

195. Where is our Rosewood? She is yet to be found standing, as she once stood.

196. Where is our Black Wall Street? She is yet to be found standing, as she once stood.

197. Must we relinquish political status, civil rights and the opportunity for higher education?

198. It has been predicted that the survival of the Negro, can only come by submission to White America.

199. Born Black and not recognized as a Woman. (Cicely Tyson)

200. Must people of color settle for disfranchisement?

201. People of color are yet prey, that's why we must pray.

202. This woman said, her husband love her so much, but she was more in love with herself than him.
203. What a befallen tragedy.

204. This ole man said, he will never see fifty again, unless the Lord gives a second try around.

205. We live with sadness, but need not sadly.

206. The brain will impulsively tell you the wrong thing to do.

207. You had better depend on your right mind.

208. Sometimes in this life, you must deviate from the norm in order to receive the Blessings of God.

209. Watch your so-called friends with your God-Given third eye.

210. There are certain things a White Man can do, but a Black Man is not-allow-to-do.

211. In the Golden Years of Life, petition the Lord for place-ment not under " *WatchCare*," but under the vibrant and self-sustaining placements of life.

212. Personal Survey: Do you smoke and chew and go with them that do? (G. A. Ladd)

213. Momma use to say, I can show your butt better than I can tell you.

214. *"Race Norming"* has become the underline factor to sys-temic discrimination.

215. If you smell sulfur burning nearby, your hater is closing-in.

216. There are too many spared rods hanging at the old wood-shed. *"Spare the rod, spoil the child."*

217. The Raccoon asked the Zebra, if he could see Friday ahead...The Zebra replied, no, there's a Camel in the way. LOL

218. TGIF and the Sunday Sabbath Day Celebration, just a day or so away.

219. Don't judge a metal can by the label. Always read the label first; to avoid opening-up a can of worms.

220. There are times when we must turn life's autopilot controls off and allow the Lord to take the wheel.

221. Jesus, take the wheel. (Carrie Underwood)

222. Allow the Lord to be your gatekeeper. Remember, we are suppose to be the sheep of His pasture.

223. Fast living brings fast *"draugh"* with *"nough."*

224. For pedestrian safety, we petitioned for street lights, but got a corralled street with concrete barriers.
225. This petition posed a systemic opportunity for a systemic degrade in the neighborhood.

226. As people of color, unwelcomed impositions are placed against us, when petitioning benefits for the masses.

227. The more change comes, the more change stays the same for people of color.

228. We ain't going back, instead, we are going forth by the hand of the Almighty God, Himself.

229. The Lord brought us, not to leave us; to lead us on.

230. Goodness and Mercy always etch a return trail back to Lord for the backslider.

231. When we were wrong, the Lord *"stood standing,"* waiting our return.

232. Satan's way is a speedway straight to Hell.

233. If you desire to revoke your Sins, just call on the Name of Jesus.

234. Avoid the Coon mentality of one speaking against another.

235. Remember, may the Lord watch between me and thee, while we are absent one from another.
236. Contrary to popular beliefs, it's the Lord taking us places, where we really don't want to go.

237. The Lord does work in mysterious ways, contrary to our beliefs and miseries.

238. God's Divinity has life and lives programmed to His "*befittings.*"

239. Satan gives us a run for our money.

240. Satan will dispute and repute, but Jesus will plea.

241. The African proverb says, a people who lack the knowledge of their past are like a tree without roots. "*Ashay.*"...Amen Lord.

242. Our struggles are marked into the treads of our Black skin.

243. Time does not dictate right, but doing right is all the time.

244. An elderly back-the-day White Woman, ask me to find her a "*Boy*" to work her garden.

245. Boy and Black does not equate any further, "*No More.*"

246. Never give up, never give in, give it all you got, without.

247. Life comes with many stipulations.
248. Money talks; everything else walks.

249. Ain't no fool, like an old fool.

250. What's Love got to do with it?

251. His behind can't stand the whipping that it needs.

252. One's personality brings out the beauty or ugliness in one's character.

253. The once recanted Black History, now brings millions of dollars in revenue to the populous.

254. One school teacher told another teacher, this Tuesday coming is February 30th. LOL

255. I know the way which they oppose.

256. Black Hope is built on "nothin" less than Jesus' Blood and His Righteousness.

257. If there ain't enough hours in your day, you need to check your Time Zone.

PROVERBIAL ESSENTIALS FOR BLACK LIVING III

1. Avoid any distractions which seek to take up room and time from your life. It's time to remove the elephant, which takes the room of your life.

2. Integrity is the best gift God has given any man. You can keep it or lose it.

3. It behooves us to never impose our agenda upon the Lord, but when we find ourselves in the midst of darkness, seek for His light.

4. Father God in Heaven, we seek your marvelous light. Lord watch over me and those, while we are absent one from another. This is our prayer through Christ Jesus, Himself, even the more.

5. When seconds matter, it is not who you can call, but it's who you can call on...and His Name is Jesus. When seconds matter, it's not who you think, but it's who you least think. Father God, with expressions of love and gratitude we come, because every second of our lives matter, as we journey each and every day which you giveth.

6. Integrity will keep you, when you can't keep yourself.

7. Steven is dead and Saul has gone crazy. Now, the Saints are scared and gone crazy too.

8. Father God in Heaven, thank You for life itself and for You giving us the portals of life, as we tread this way. Now, we celebrate Your Goodness with expressions of love and gratitude, as we pray.

9. By the allowance of the Almighty God and without any discretions, death is thereby summoned with its sting to disrobe us all of what we here possess. Be reminded, Momma would say, be ready, when He comes.

10. Maintain your integrity and it shall keep you.

11. Momma would say, every dog got his day. Be careful how you treat others.

12. We all have a scheduled appointment with death.

13. If you have the Will, God has the way.

14. Invest in yourself and the Lord will invest in you.

15. We are living in trying times, when men and women, boys and girls can't see the forest for the trees. Have Mercy Lord, have Mercy, *"cause"* Mercy best suits all our cases.

16. If you are of the Lord's, the oil will flow and pour upon your life.

17. When it's from the heart, your Yes, Sir and Yes, Madam goes a long ways; all the way from earth to Heaven and back

from Heaven to earth; working for your good on earth.

18. It's a Blessing when God's answer to prayer is no.

19. The Book of Daniel teaches us how to do right, instead of wrong. When King Darius peeked into the lions' den, I can read the mind of Daniel. *"I am still here O' King... You meant it for Evil, but God meant it for good, O' King Darius."*

20. Sometimes, we must go through Hell to rule in Heavenly places.

21. Sometimes, we must go through Hell to reach Heaven.

22. Based on John 3:16, I have a presupposed right to hate, but instead, I so loved. I have cracks in my Black, because of imposed endurances, due to my skin color.

23. As your Faith increases, the need for evidence decreases. Otherwise, you learn to walk by Faith, not by sight.

24. This little toddler woke up and came out of her bedroom with sleep still in her eyes; she said, Grandma? Grandma said, Yes baby. The little girl said, Grandma, you are the best Grandma and a good cooker too. It's most apparent that she wanted Grandma to cook breakfast for her.

25. Greatness is small things, done well.

26. The case of the *"Issue of Blood"*....Well *"who touched*

me?"

27. Reach out and touch Him.

28. As students in elementary school, we always wanted to know what goes on in a teacher's lounge. After tipping down the hall, we would push the lounge door wide open and run the hardest to avoid being caught. Now, that I am a teacher, I refuse to go in a teacher's lounge. Don't want see nor talk to anybody.

29. If you are a child of God, the best come with the latter of the story. Ask Ole Man Job.

30. Don't let Satan defeat you. Your story ain't over, until the Fat Lady sings. It's a guaranteed, that she will never show up to sing.

31. You can be in church every Sunday and never touch God.

32. She suffered twelve long years. She was label an outcast by the church and folks did not like her, because of her bloody sickness. Yet, Jesus came along and went back to the beginning of her twelve long years, healed and made her whole again.

33. Jesus always goes back and makes whole from the beginning of your brokenness.

34. Likewise, He always does more than you ask. The issue was not the blood, but the issue was to be made whole.

35. The lame man at the pool: Sometimes, we don't even recognize Jesus being right there in our midst, because we stay in complaint mode all the time. *"Sir, I have no man, when the water is troubled, to put me into the pool."*

36. The lame man failed to answer the question posed by Jesus. We have the same bad habit.

37. The lame man failed, because of a lack of listening, ignorance, and the blame game.

38. An Old Saint of a Nun said, she does not like hash, no matter how it's cook. She would say, hash is hash, even when it comes to our everyday living. A scrambled life makes cooked hash.

39. Jesus is on the Mainline; tell Him, what you want.

40. If you have not realized it, your computer spell check does not want the *"S"* for Satan capitalized. It takes my computer three times to keep the *"S"* capitalized on Satan.

41. I rebuke him right now in the name of Jesus, the Christ.

42. Satan's name needs to be capitalized, so I can see him coming.

43. Life is a funny thing. Just make sure you stay in your lane, if not you may suffer severe consequences of lane changing.

44. Yet, if you decide to lane change, make sure Goodness and Mercy are in your rearview mirror.

45. Someone heard one old fellow saying, "*It don't git no gooder than this*"...that is with Jesus on your side.

46. Call Him up and tell Him what you want.

47. Be reminded, prayer goes where phone lines can't go; even to the jailhouse.

48. Satan has deputized demons called, IMPS.

49. IMPS are Satan's warfare warriors.

50. Being Black is an EXPERIENCE.

51. As a child of God, in the midst of troubles, I may be grounded, but still flying.

52. For some, hate and hostility has become a way of living, without actual living.

53. Last Sunday, a member asked the deacon where was his wife and how was she doing? The deacon replied, "*She is prayerful today.*" Meaning, she ain't coming to church this morning.

54. By being Black, we are the black on the pepper.

55. This elderly man told me that he wakes up every morning laughing. He said, all because he beat death at his game one more day.

56. The older Grandma gets, the more she worries about making it to the next day.

57. Jesus told His disciples the same thing which my Momma told me. I will not be with you always. Then and then only did the disciples know, something did not sound right.

58. The Devil is crouching at your front door. Ask Abel, Cain's brother. Don't hate on me.

59. It's not how much we give, but how much love we put into our giving. Now, it's known why the Lord loves cheerful givers.

60. Buy a Brother or Sister some cheer through your caring and sharing; even in your giving.

61. This old country preacher said, the see through glass pulpit was the cheaper-kind of pulpit and he was worried that it might be magnifying him to the congregation.

62. Saints and People of God, don't get weary in well doing.

63. As Black Folk, we fight every day for everything.

64. When it comes to the Color of the skin, remember the words of Jesus. All these things will they do unto you for my

name sake, because they know not Him who sent me.

65. When folk hate on you, because of your skin color, they don't know the Lord God Himself.

66. Give the Lord a Big Shout-out!!!

67. The Undertaker is the first and the last responder to last Enemy called, Death.

68. Learn to improve and make a change.

69. The purpose of teaching is to engage your people; the audience, children, congregation, listeners or students.

70. Lord, we know you are the beginning and the end; only to have your way, even the more...

71. No matter how long you live, life is still short.

72. It takes tons of energy to look ugly and mean spirited towards others.

73. Ole Man Job said, our days are few and full of trouble. Avoid being a bearer of trouble on others.

74. When we get to the gates of Heaven, St. Peter will ask us to give him our access number. Give him the same access number used for your credit union account.

75. After their house of straw was blown down, one of the three little pigs said, let's buy brick. Except the Lord build the house, they labor in vain that *"buildeth"* it.

76. The New Normal is to love the Lord, even that He may be glorified and we may be satisfied.

77. Sometimes, we are despised, but not forsaken.

78. Black lives depend on your vote at the ballot.

79. Old folk would say, I got the Monday Blues.

80. Why would you allow willful Sin to forfeit the Blessings of the Lord upon your life?

81. Ain't nothing wrong with celebrating 2021, because 2020 came with a *"cumberson"* load of cares.

82. Applied knowledge is most powerful in the Black Community

83. Know your circles of influence.

84. Beware, the content of your character is being weighed.

85. Daddy use to say, I am getting stiff; now at my age, that's well understood.

86. Oh, my big toe; it's going to rain.

87. No matter what, ever little bit helps.

88. Penny saved, penny earned. *"clare"* before God, the truth.

89. A collaboration of Gender and Race brings forth peace for all generations to come.

90. The Colored Women Federation Club brought us thus far.

91. Back in the day, little Colored Girls played with White Baby dolls.

92. There were no Black Baby dolls to be had... God's timing brought change for our girls.

93. As the Old Folk would say, *"just keep living."*

94. Death cometh from whence we know not and *"goeth"* where we know not.

95. Death is our last enemy. His name is the *"Grim Reaper."*

96. If anybody should know death, the Undertaker ought to...

97. FUNERAL: This ain't the end. One day, each of us are coming back to the church house as a broken sealed empty envelope.

98. In spite of death... to stay here, God is with us; to go there, we are with God.

99. The world believes that Blacks are smart; I Believe Blacks are smarter.

100. Why do they play our music in stores?

101. Why do they play our music to promote commercial ads?

102. The agility of your Black is being weighed everyday throughout this world.

103. The pandemic of 2020 was induced by the forces of Evil to apprehend lives with no matter.

104. Everybody sees the world from the hole in the fence.

105. Only the Lord can see the world from abroad and above.

106. As a boy, Black maids cleaned White houses. *"Black maids." "White houses."* What contrast?

107. Lord, we thank you for making a way, where there was no way.

108. The New Normal is to have a little talk with Jesus.

109. Tell Him about all your struggles. He will hear your faintest cry.

110. The New Normal shall be a time for God's People to rejoice in Him, even the more.

111. Old Folk said, *"He is no shorter than His Word."*

112. Talk to the Devil and talk against his evilness, brings forth victory. Satan, I rebuke you Demon.

113. One news reporter declared politics to have a bully pulpit against people of color.

114. If you ever wanted your children to hear you, just whisper with softness. It works.

115. If you ever have issues with life, get into the presence of God and YOU will get straighten out. GUARANTEED RE-SULTS.

116. NOTICE: Satan always ask questions of you and quiz you concerning God's perfect Will for you.

117. Though it all, times teaches us to wait on the Lord.

118. God's waiting room is one of the hardest waiting rooms to wait-inside of...

119. Ole Man Job said, if I could just talk to you Lord, then, I can tell you my side of the story.

120. Have you ever wanted to talk to the Lord? Have you ever wanted to see his handy hand?

121. Again, He is no shorter than His Word.

122. Mother Wit told Black Folk to pull cotton, while the dew was still out for a heavier weigh at the scales.

123. Known is an elderly lady laying on her bed of languishing; unknowingly, she is picking the threads in the carpet for the cotton in fields.

124. There is no Social Distancing with the Lord; "*Nearer to Thee*," I want to be......

125. Bad or good, do your best which the Lord Himself expects of you.

126. The New Normal has posed dim shadows of the Jim Crow upon God's People.

127. When matter is deleted out of life, there is no life left for living.

128. Jesus lived to die, so we can die to live.

129. Life sometimes has staggering consequences beyond our limitations.

130. Life does change suddenly by the loosing of life.

131. Sometimes life poses unsuspecting odds against us, but Jesus has a way of turning the tables over.

132. Shadowed beneath Thy Hand, may we forever stand; true

to God, true to our Native Land.

133. Learn to live life. Change comes with living. Create your own ambitions.

134. Jesus Himself, knows all our griefs and sorrows.

135. God leads, but we have a choice to let Him lead.

136. The Old Folk said, He never lost a case.

137. Your personal complaint ain't against me as you think, but against God. (Exodus 15:8)

138. What in Hell Do You Want?

139. As a boy, Momma would say, the people in Hell want ice water.

140. Even after God does so much for us, we rather still live in Hell and like Hell.

141. Some folk like misery. Some folk ain't living, unless they have misery for their friend.

142. The same God, my Lord and your Lord. (Exodus 15:8)

143. We are guilty as charged for frustrating the Grace of God by the hollow of our Sinful feet.

144. The Lord will make way even, while we are raising Hell and looking ugly.

145. Some can't see the forest for the trees.

146. Trusting God makes good our living by faith.

147. Hearken unto His voice.

148. Do that which is right in His sight.

149. Give an ear to His Commandments.

150. Keep His Statutes.

151. Hope and hopelessness contends in a tug-of-war for our Faith.

152. It was Satan who posted a 2020 pandemic against the church.

153. And *"when it came to pass"*, the Lord had already brought me through.

154. Adversity was defeated as He brought me through.

155. Cast your cares upon Him; for He is a Mighty Catcher.

156. Black Folk can't hardly buy now, what was once thrown away food for the slaves.

157. What about the chitterlings?

158. What about the turnips greens with the roots still on them?

159. What about neck bones and salt pork?

160. Within the Valley of the Shadows of Death, our George Floyd cried out.

161. His despised death broke silence throughout the world.

162. He cried Mother! Through the timing tones of his death.

163. Jesus too, cried out Mother! Behold thy son.

164. His despised death broke silence throughout the world too.

165. Let it be known, every night before bed, I take the knee.

166. These are my uttered words, Father, lay me down to sleep; *"Bless my Soul to keep."*

167. What God has for me; it's for me.

168. Satan knows your address and agenda.

169. Satan looks to find the hedges which should be around your life.

170. Satan said, you have a hedge around him, around his house, and around all he hath.

171. Where is your hedge? If you have one, let it grow high and tall.

172. The overweight doctor told his patient to do as I say, not as I do.

173. Trouble always has a way of finding you.

174. Jesus Himself, will turn tables for you that He may receive the Glory.

175. Life is as we know it, but living comes on the other side of death.

176. In bereavement, always share your empathy and sympathy to the bereaved.

177. Empathy from your inner being of caring; sympathy from your outward display of sharing.

178. Death has an untimely way of intruding and interrupting our schedules.

179. The question was posed: If a man die, shall he live again?

180. Ole Man Job was very inquisitive about this thing called, death.

181. His answer got hung-up in a cloud.

182. His question was 2000 years ahead of his time. That's why it was hung up in a cloud.

183. With an unreturned answer to himself; Job said, though He slay me, yet will I trust Him.

184. Satan was the slaying culprit; only at the Lord's perfect disposal.

185. Life circumstances will cause us to think pass the capacities of life.

186. A Rich White Man wished he could have paid a poor Black Man to take his surgery.

187. Be it known rich or poor, every tub must set on its on bottom sooner than later.

188. Riches and money can you take you lots of places, but not everywhere.

189. Then on the other hand, riches and money will take you, where you wished... you had not gone.

190. Life as we know it has a beginning and ending; an arrival

and departure.

191. Yet, we find ourselves somewhere in between.

192. An unannounced death of a love-one is never forthcoming.

193. Death is the art of dying. For to live is Christ; to die is gain.

194. Death does not allow us to circumvent the rules.

195. Death of a beloved-one consummates the realities of life.

196. Death breaks hearts with tears and weeping.

197. We spend all our years as a tale that is told; our tale is part of His story.

198. There will be a Heaven and a Hell.

199. Sometimes it's good to remodify our question, when we are quizzing the Lord.

200. It's is a good thing, when you know for fact the Lord has vested interest in you.

201. It's an amazing thing to trust the Lord in a dying hour.

202. In all the days of my appointed times, I am going to wait

on the Lord.

203. All of us are living daily between the crevices of sickness, dying and death.

204. Again, we all have an appointed hour of death, soon to come.

205. The hymn writer declared that death will soon disrobe us all of what we here possess.

206. Jesus was hanging between two thieves with dying and death in the balance.

207. Death and the grave became instigators in attempt to seize His body.

208. It's a good thing when you can turn your head to the wall for prayer like King Hezekiah.

209. Our Samone Biles and Henry *"Hank"* Aaron came through woes and foes.

210. Skin color was the demonstrated culprit on display.

211. The Lord will intentionally allow us to be put down to bring us up a better way.

212. Many times the unwanted way is least expected, but better.

213. Momma would say, "Boy come here, I *"wanna"* learn you something.

214. What she meant: Boy, I want to teach you something.

215. Auntee use to say, the Lord done bought us from a mighty long ways.

216. We must learn to ponder on those things, which we do not immediately understand.

217. Ponder means in good Faith, not to walk blindly on your own.

218. Ponder means in good Faith, to walk step-by-step with the leading of the Lord.

219. Ponder means in good Faith, search for wisdom, while allowing wisdom to speak.

220. There is a spiritual intelligence surrounding us every mega second.

221. There is a cosmic warfare going-on over our heads; Satan verses the Angels of God.

222. Decrease that He may increase.

223. Decrease that you may receive the increase.

224. It is believed, Dr. Clay Evans said, there is room at the cross.

225. There is a Blessing in your pressing.

226. Make good of your living.

227. The Lord has a Divine Habit of doing more, than what we originally asked of Him.

228. I know the way of the righteous, but the way of ungodly shall perish.

229. Ole Man Job wants us to know that our Redeemer, "*Liveth.*"

230. When we are born, we are ahead of time. Yet, at some point in life, time passes us.

231. "*A Mind is a Terrible Thing to Waste.*" (UNCF)

232. When death done sat-in, the Soul has got to move to a better place.

233. The Lord retrieves back, what belongs to Him.

234. When death done sat-in, Eternal living takes over for the believer.

235. The hymn writer says, death will soon disrobe us all of

what we here possess.

236. Death leaves us in repose as an empty brown envelope.

237. Precious in the sight of Lord is the death of His Saints. (Psalms 116:15)

238. Death becomes a junction point.

239. Death becomes a transition point.

240. Death becomes a connecting point, between mortality, a Believer's immortality.

241. The Lord sometimes moves us from pain to purpose. Then from purpose to power.

242. Believers are sometimes *"Takin a lickin,"* while coming out *"kickin."*

243. At birth, new born babies take a *"lickin,"* then come out *"kickin."*

244. The Old COGIC Saints, while in the midst of praying, would say, Yes Lord! Yes Lord!

245. They would cry out, Even the more Lord, Even the more...

246. Then they would say, I am a Soldier of the Cross.

247. Saved, Sanctified, Holy Ghost filled, Fire Baptized... got a mind to run on and see what the end *"gonna"* be like.

248. Your ability will not bring peace and tranquility to your situation.

249. Society has hindered our ability to take on the mind of Christ.

250. Digital technology and social media have dictated our thinking towards spiritual living.

251. We must learn to utilize mind control.

252. Seize the moment. Be all that you can become.

253. We must integrate our thoughts and energies through the power of daily mediation.

254. When we hope, it changes the structure of the brain to immigrate to a positive sector.

255. Without Faith, we cannot please the Lord.

256. Faith is an element by which we can alter the physical structure of the brain.

257. Try speaking to your storm. Maybe, it will behave.

258. Life is what you make it, regardless.

259. Think little, be little.

260. Think BIG, be BIG...

261. You are what you think all day long.

262. Thinking manifest reality.

263. Hope becomes reality only when reality becomes the dream.

264. We don't have to steal, just ask.

265. Have not, because we ask not.

266. The more you give, the more you shall receive. God's standard for everyday living.

267. A tight fist cannot receive.

268. Just maybe, the Lord is telling you something.

269. Why do wrong, when right is there?

270. Why even choose wrong, when you can have right?

271. Right develops self-integrity.

272. Availability is what the Lord ask of us.

273. Make sure, you know in whom you Believe.

274.Times are reflecting drastic changes; to exclude the very existence of people of color.

275. Only the strong shall survive. That is the strong in the Lord.

276. Make sure your anchor holds.

277. Make sure the ground, which you are standing is not sinking sand.

278. Only prayer changes people. Only you can change things.

279. Be the book which everybody reads. Become that Best-selling book.

280. Seek Godly counsel when needed. Never counsel yourself, because Satan hears.

281. Be all that you can be for the Lord. The Lord wants you in His Army.

282. Not only does Uncle Sam wants you, but the Lord too.

283. The way of the ungodly shall perish, provided an immediate right turns is made.

284. Holiness is beautiful in the eyes of the beholder.

285. Count your Blessings; bet you will never finish counting. Man's Blessings are infinite.

286. Seek Him and Him only.

287. One lady complained of her lack, but then failed to realize what was in her possession.

288. We see our losses, but never count our gains.

289. An idle mind is the Devil's workshop for a human disaster.

290. Maybe, Humpty Dumpty broke into pieces, but God specializes in broken pieces.

291. Have you ever been an accident going to happen? Well, in life...Click it or ticket it.

292. Successes and failures in life depend upon your perception of success and failure.

293. Sometimes, we knowingly or unknowingly sleep with the Devil.

294. When the Devil makes your bed, you have no choice, but sleep in tears.

295. There is Soulful learning in the midst of Black Colleges and Universities.

296. Be all you can be, and nothing no less than *"Thee"* best. God's best.

297. Prayer is worth lots of money, when you need it the most.

298. The worth of prayer cannot be paid through a purchased price.

299. The Lord is looking for a few good soldiers in His Army.

300. Be all that you can be in the Army of the Lord.

301. The Old Church of God in Christ, *"Got my war shoes on in the Army of the Lord."*

302. Momma would say, the Lord ain't no shorter than His Word.

303. She would say, if you take one step, the Lord will take two steps.

304. Two to one ain't bad, when you need the Lord the most.

305. Call Him up and tell Him what you want, cause He is an on time God.

306. He's an on time God, yes, He is...

307. God is good all the time; all the time He is good.

308. You can't go wrong with Jesus.

309. He is a Rock in A Weary Land; a shelter in the time of a storm.

310. Make sure you are holding on to your *"holt."*

311. The very best part of waking up is coffee in your cup and a mind stayed on Jesus Christ.

312. Ain't nothing bad about a homeless shelter; Jesus said, the Son of Man has nowhere to lay His head.

313. If you find yourself displaced, at least you are not on your face.

314. Those who care, give and share; they may reap the benefits of life's longevity.

315. Those that are persistently in Worship Services may reap life's longevity.

316. Forsake not thyself from the assembly of the Saints, that you may stay strong in the Lord.

317. Those that seek me early, shall find me. (Proverbs 8:17)

318. The Lord ain't hard to find; seek Him out.

319. Be not anxious for nothing, but in all things pray, till the

Lord answers.

320. His answer might be yes, no, or wait awhile.

321. Jesus in the morning, Jesus at noonday, Jesus at night.

322. This world cannot afford us a home.

323. Your life is the life, which the Lord gives; your body belongs to the Lord for Himself.

324. The temple of the Holy Ghost awaits inside of your Soul.

325. Have your way Jesus, have your way. I am the clay, you are the potter; God is the potters' wheel.

326. Be humble and honor will come to you.

327. Be obedient and favor will come too.

328. Look on others and others will look on you.

329. Time always tells the story, whether good or bad.

330. Don't think you can get away; wherever you are God's there too...ask Jonah.

331. Done in the dark, shines in the light.

332. No forged weapon against you shall prosper.

333. Seek favor, not hate.

334. *"Buked and scorned;"* call everything except a child of God. Just wait on time.

335. Time knows and documents the situation. Vengeance is mine *"sayeth"* the Lord.

336. That's why Momma says, the Lord knows. *"Theirs' a comin."*

337. Be careful who you hate on. It will come back and bite you miserably.

338. The Lord looks out for His own.

339. You can't go wrong *"wit"* the Lord on your side. I *"clare fore"* God.

340. Hold you head up high in spite of what's going on in your life. God will sustain.

341. When life got you down, lotion your face and keep going.

342. When I would slow poke, Daddy would say, *"git"* a move on you."

343. Sometimes, all we need is a move on us.

344. Think about this one: Momma always said, Son never

send a woman to college.

345. Many *"a"* men have lost wives after providing them opportunities to attend college.

346. Think about this one too: Momma said, always go in business by yourself; not with someone else.

347. Momma didn't raise a fool.

348. Know yourself, before trying to know somebody else.

349. The way you dress, tells the rest.

350. Always, dress for success.

351. Being people of color, it has been said, *"we live in a Don't Shoot society"*.

352. *"Hands Up, Don't Shoot"*.

353. You will never know the end, until you have endure to the end.

354. The Old Black Saints wept tears, but made endurance a way of life; till the Lord said, *"well done."*

355. Life ain't a mystery; neither a wonder, it's for real. Bad or good, it's for real.

356. Jesus lived to die, so we can die to live.

357. Regardless, Mother Nature and Father Time, takes their toll on our lives.

358. Our fallen nature and Satan's behavior has caused this Evil upon us.

359. Ask yourself, if there is junk in your trunk?

360. You can't pass Godly inspection with junk in your trunk.

361. Lots of us can't pray straight, because we have junk-in-the-trunk.

362. Lay-a-side every weight and Sin that so easily beset us.

363. That you may pray straight.

364. According to the scriptures, questions posed to Jesus were redirected back as a questions to the persons asking them.

365. Surely, He is a lawyer in a courtroom.

366. Yet, His question to us...Is there anything too hard for me?

367. Time is always on the side of the Believer.

368. If you have life, sooner or later, you will find rest.

369. I have faced far worst with less.

370. Are you waiting till the 13th hour?

371. Old folk used to say, boy you made it by the skin of your teeth.

372. If some of us make it to Heaven, it will be by the skin of our teeth.

373. Lots of us think we are going to Heaven anyhow. If you get there, it will be anyhow.

374. Ole Man Job *"learned"* me something. There is skin on our teeth.

375. WARNING: There is a risky danger of losing out on Heaven.

376. If you make it into Heaven by the skin of your teeth, it's better than, not making it at all.

377. The arrogant dying thief on the cross was waiting for the 13th hour to come. Maybe, a bit too late.

378. The good thief was on His right side. The right side signifies righteousness.

379. The bad thief was on the left side. The left side signifies wandering and waiting.

380. Waiting for that 13th hour did not acquit the verdict of guilty.

381. Death was in a race against the 13th hour; the 13th hour could not hold up death.

382. A military commander told his soldiers, *"don't pee dirty,"* it will end your career.

383. Bankrupted twice, divorced twice, broke, and slept in his car behind the building; *"Yet"?*

384. Old Folk would say, child the Lord will make a way, somehow.

385. I don't want any stank on my hands; trying to go home to see the Lord.

386. God works in cycles and seasons.

387. I have a Father that pays child support.

388. Think it not strange, when ye fall into divers temptations

389. Job saw the hands of God, along with His Mighty workings.

390. Some of the Old Black Saints would pawn their shot guns to get milk for the baby.

391. The Lord brought us, when we could not bring ourselves.

392. So why do you act like Mr. BIG STUFF?

393. Maybe, you are stuffed with the wrong stuff.

394. The Glory of God is what should keep us filled, that we should hunger no more.

395. That we should thirst no more, neither.

396. Wisdom is having a lots to say, but hardly saying it.

397. Wisdom is engaging into complete silence while exercising quiet time.

398. Wisdom is learning to listen during your quiet time.

399. There are times when we know where we are...but not where we are going.

400. It's bad thing to get to your destination and not know to get off.

401. Joshua and Caleb spying out the promise land and presenting it before the church.

402. The first church business meeting was tabled with failure to trust in the promise.

403. They had the deeds, but failed to possess the land.

404. In the church house, you may get called everything, except a child of God.

405. In the church house, you may get hated on...

406. I declare, when I desire to do good, Evil is always present.

407. While running from the mice, remember the Lord is our mice trap.

408. Depression minus a few alphabets, becomes an everyday word of pressed-on

409. Maybe, it becomes **PRESSED-ON** with the *"ed"* reversed from *"de."*

410. We are pressed on from every side day-by-day.

411. Real vision allows us to live by Faith.

412. Real Faith allows us to live by vision.

413. Vengeance is mine sayeth the Lord God Almighty.

414. The human eyes are the light to one's Soul.

415. Have you ever wondered, why folk drop their heads when talking to others?

416. There is story to be told; good or bad.

417. Don't die with a book inside of you.

418. Folks can see your Soul through the eyes.

419. Your eyes are critical to who you are and what you possess.

420. Have you ever wonder how people can spot a liar or scammer?

421. Eyes can acquit, or convict.

422. That's why lady justice wears a *"doo rag"*; so she can't read eyes.

423. She should listen to the evidence and not peek.

424. Many times, when it comes to people of color, she peeks from the *"doo rag."*

425. Do good and Good will follow while holding the hand of his friend, Mercy.

426. You might put your shoes on in the morning, but somebody else might take them off in the evening.

427. At death, you might have instructions for everybody, but no real say so in the matter.

428. All of Job's life, he heard of God, but trials actually introduced him to God.

429. Afterwards, Job knew Him for himself.

430. Momma use to say, boy, you had better know the Lord for yourself.

431. That's why, sooner or later, every tub must sit on its own bottom.

432. We had a number 1 tub, a number 2 tub and a number 3 tub. Those were the days.

433. Hearing of the Lord by the ear ain't enough. Job confessed his dilemma.

434. That's the way it works in our lives. It takes troubles to introduce us to God.

435. All things "*worketh*" together for introduction of the Lord to the center stage of your life.

436. We must go through hard times for the Lord to press the wrinkles out of us.

437. That's why the Lord says, he is coming for a church without spot or wrinkles.

438. Salvation cleans the spots out; pressing takes the wrinkles out.

439. Good or bad, whatever you are doing will bring you to your harvest.

440. A bad crop or a good crop.

441. Whatever so a man "*soweth*" that shall he also reap. Watch which kind of seeds you are broadcasting.

442. I am determined not to know anything among you saved Jesus Christ and Him, crucified.

443. Casting and reeling. Cast your bread upon the waters and in many days, it shall return.

444. It comes back when you least expect.

445. It comes back when you need it the most.

446. By Faith, cast what you need the most from the Lord. It shall return in a due season.

447. Today's church folks Believe in the Old Testament. Eye for an eye, tooth for a tooth.

448. When sickness, dying and death comes forth, a new life of Eternal Salvation takes place.

449. Nothing else in this world matters, when you are laying upon a dying bed.

450. Sometimes ain't nothing else you can do, except cry when the world gives a counterfeit.

451. A well-known movie star said, if he could do life over, it would be different.

452. The Ole Saints use to "sang," I don't know why, I have to cry "*sometime*." Yes, sometime.

453. Hezekiah disconnected from this world and made himself a prayer closet at the wall.

454. He made himself a Hebrew "*Weeping Wall*."

455. The Bible suggest, he wept sore with blood shot eyes from the severity of his situation.

456. Pending death changes agendas and schedules; nothing in life matters any more.

457. Death carries a permanent sting like none other.

458. Never accept what you don't want to accept.

459. Never let others establish your premise.

460. Trials and tribulations can only do two things; break you

or remake you.

461. When life causes you to capsize, call on the one who stilled the waters and winds.

462. Afterwards, somebody said, even the winds and waves obeyed.

463. Sometimes, we are too mean to live and unfit to die.

464. Science tells us nothing about the speed of prayer and its worth.

465. Tears, plus prayers vent. This initiates the Lord to hear and listen to your faintest cry.

466. Jesus saw that His death was imminent; the scene played over and over for thirty-three years.

467. Sweat like drops of blood ran down as he prayed the tolerance of His own death.

468. Job's question from over 2000 years ago had to be answered. If a man die, shall he...?

469. Death wanted Jesus, but dying would not release Him.

470. Death begged dying to release Him into his custody.

471. Then the grave got into the competition for His body by

rebuking dying and death.

472. The grave begged dying and death to let Him be released into his custody.

473. The grave assured dying and death that he could hold Him in the grave, without a lost.

474. Now, you know the rest of the story.

475. Well, Job's answer to his question finally came. *"If a man die, shall he live again?"*

476. In all my appointed time, I am going wait, till my change come.

477. We tend to major in the minor and minor in the major.

478. When we can't trace His hands, always trust His Heart.

479. He has a heart that's driven to Love.

480. There are times in life, when we really don't know why. Yet, God knows.

481. Inward deception keep us bound in the fantasy of Sin.

482. Human ego brings on Sin. Sin brings on death.

483. Death brings Eternal destruction.

484. Each day you live, there is an opportunity for you to preach your trial sermon.

485. Folks will hate on you anyhow; especially family.

486. We have every right to hate; instead we love, because He first loved. (John 3:16).

487. Whether by bullet or prison, the lives of Black are being incarcerated daily.

488. *"Hands up, don't shoot."* A familiar cry in the midst of undue street justice.

489. As we think, we change the physical nature of our brain progression.

490. Your thinking and the power of your thinking can change reality for the better or worst.

491. There must be a daily routine of renewing our minds to possess the same mind of Jesus.

492. Our thoughts are real and cannot be discarded; they are filed in the subconscious.

493. We emit energy here on earth and in Heaven, based upon our thinking.

494. We bind and loose here on earth and in Heaven, based

upon what we think the most.

495. Can't win for losing; just keep losing then...

496. If it ain't one thing, it's another. Wait, another one is coming.

497. "*The Devil is busy.*" Well, just keep giving him the glory.

498. If it wasn't for bad luck, I wouldn't have any luck at all. Lucky you.

499. Our thinking was shattered in the Garden of Eden.

500. This unknown man in Atlanta, constantly praised the Lord under his breathe all-the-day-long.

501. You are what you think all day long; regardless.

502. I am, I have, I know, I am certain, good follows me always; only good lays before me.

503. The powers of earth and Heaven are at the command of your thinking.

504. Life is according to the power that "*worketh*" in you.

505. Faith alters the physical structure of the brain and its ability to manifest results.

506. We are to think through things one-at-a-time.

507. Our brain creates folds like a rolodex; bad or good. It's your call.

508. The Lord requires designed thinking on our part.

509. Think on the things which are lovely, pure, just and of good report.

510. Quality mediations keep us aligned with God's way of thinking for our good.

511. Reach out beyond where you are at the moment. She said, if I could, but touch the hem of His garment.

512. First, there must be an active reach within your mind.

513. Our minds need time to understand, what the Holy Spirit already knows.

514. We must learn to set forth the standards of provision, which God has already laid out for us.

515. And this too shall pass...

516. The other day, I told Satan, tricks are for kids and amateurs.

517. As He walked the dusty roads of Palestine, His death

replayed scene after scene.

518. I was once young, now I am old. Never seen the righteous forsaken, neither his seed begging bread.

519. This wife told her husband, if you shoot a gun the way you pee, we are in deep trouble.

520. It's *"hellashish"* when the husband sends the girlfriend to take his wife shopping.

521. Safety is of the Lord.

522. The most dangerous thing in a war zone is an indecisive military officer.

523. A double minded man is unstable in all his ways.

524. Jesus said, lift me up and I will do the drawing. Avoid arguing with your spouse.

525. We as people of color have failed to dig deep enough for the gold.

526. We want the gold, but too complacent to dig for the gold.

527. The digital age has disconnected mankind from the realities of a True and Living God.

528. Two things God cannot do. He cannot lie and He cannot fail.

529. There is a Godly call on your life. Reach for it.

530. Never think you can take comfort in what the Lord, DID NOT bless.

531. A blind man can see God's Goodness and never see his own hands.

532. Be ye angry, but Sin not. Let not the sun go down upon your wrath.

533. Well, there is a brand new remedy to one's madness after the sun goes down. What?

534. After the sun goes down and you are still mad, stay up all night long without sleeping.

535. A wise son, "*Maketh*" a glad father.

536. God's Goodness is a place of abode and refuge with the sure essence of His nature.

537. Life is not about how much you know, but about how much you really don't know.

538. He will give us the desires of our hearts.

539. At the end of preaching his sermon, the preacher always feels like a *"Full Gospel"* preacher.

540. A woman called in on the radio and asked, what should she do? I have the case of two boyfriends and I love both of them.

541. You can't love and serve two masters at the same.

542. In the case of the two boyfriends, holding a come to Jesus meeting might be the best thing to do.

543. If you cheated for it...it ain't good.

544. If you stole for it ...it ain't good.

545. If you lied for it ...it ain't good.

546. If you played tricks for it...it ain't good.

547. All good and perfect gifts come from above.

548. Life is an illusion, death is reality.

549. After the funeral, Black Folk will eat-up all the Fried Chicken and Collard Greens at the repast and forget the deceased ever lived.

550. Afterwards, they belch and then, you are soon forgotten.

551. Hosea had a wife who did not want to be kept.

552. If somebody does not want to be kept, best to turn them loose.

553. You had better hold on to what you got.

554. Stood for nothing, fell for everything.

555. Brokenness will bring you back to the Lord.

556. Is it true that a heart ain't good for nothing, but to be broken?

557. Avoid getting syrupy on the Lord. Now, ain't the time for a "*meltdown.*"

558. Some of us kill the proof, when we fail to share our testimony to others.

559. Maybe, we all need a Soulful overhaul.

560. Even the mosquitoes Believe, there is a wonder working power in the Blood.

561. Never think you are a **BIG DOG**, because a little dog may bring you down.

562. Snooze and you will lose.

563. Momma said, all the preacher do is lie, lie, and lie every Sunday by saying, we ain't *"gonna"* be long this morning.

564. The Black preacher will say, give me five more minutes. The five more minutes never, ever come.

565. The human Soul is susceptible to any kinds of spiritual diseases.

566. There's not a Friend like the Lowly Jesus:

567. No, not one! No, not one!

568. None else could heal all our Souls' diseases:

569. Jesus knows all about our struggles:

570. He will guide, till the day is done.

571. You see my glory, but don't know my story.

572. We as people, live so deeply inside of ourselves, till others can't reach down far enough to pull us out.

573. The funeral is the aboding place of the grim reaper, called Death.

574. If anyone should know the face of death, the Undertaker should know, beyond any shadows of doubt.

575. It's a serious taboo for a guest to sit at the head of some-body else dinner table, unless asked by host.

576. Sin has become the worth of winking at with one eye.

577. Sin has become a platform for illicit and most ungodli-ness, which nets celebrity status.

578. Sin has become a multimillion dollars platform through-out the world.

579. Sin has become an entertainment venue, which pleases the eyes and ears.

580. Sin has virtually forfeited *"Amazing Grace,"* the National Black Anthem of the Church.

581. We were blinded and we are still blind by the effects SIN.

582. All have Sinned and come short.

583. Not you all, but all have Sinned and come short.

584. Holiness is the way of earthly living in the presence of a Living God.

585. Some stuff, we ought to leave alone before it fester on us.

586. Sin will fester, while causing infection, pain and suffering with heartaches.

587. Momma use to say, "*Boy, learn some sense.*"

588. Sense is hard to learn, until you have suffered the undue pains.

589. Play with fire; get burned.

590. One thief on the cross with Jesus, owned-up to his faults, while the other refused to own-up.

591. Sometimes, our smartness will make us look like a blame fool, as Momma would say.

592. After Jesus' encounter with death. The question was asked, how can He, be the one...?

593. It's always best to be on the right side of Jesus. There His Righteousness abides.

594. On God's right is where He sat in Heaven. Does that not tell you to be on His right side?

595. Still, His three hour encounter with death chimed the question, how can He be the one?

596. Fear will make Evil folks hush-up, when terror strikes the scene.

597. Prayers and tears go together.

598. God interprets tears and prayers.

599. I have been to the gates of Hell and back.

600. God does the work as we give Him all the praise.

601. Wisdom is learned by the learner.

602. Wisdom is learned through personal experiences.

603. Wisdom is learned through the experiences of others.

604. Wisdom is learned through the Word of God.

605. Learning is the subject, when pain is the teacher of the lesson.

606. Mothers of Color no longer have "Wit;" it has become extinct in the Black Culture.

607. Death hides himself within the crevices of our shadow.

608. I can hear David saying, I am walking through the valley of the shadow of death.

609. David knew he and Death walked within the same shared shadow, without seeing each other.

610. Both David and Death casted their shadows without any separation.

611. Death lives in shadows of obscurity, because he is our last enemy.

612. Sometimes his presence is felt; other times not felt.

613. If his darkness was revealed to our natural eyes, we would exemplify our readiness.

614. I Love them that love me; those that seek me early shall find me.

615. Our position should be to-do-well by the Lord, so He may do-well-by us.

616. And by this, shall all men know that you are mine.

617. And I think to myself, *"what a wonderful world."* Despite his struggles with racism.

618. ONLY Racist People, practice racism.

619. The Lord keeps a master plan in spite of our endured situations.

620. Satan meant it for Evil, but God meant it for good.

621. He is a Demon

622. He is a Devil

623. He Demises

624. Have you ever been lost and then found?

625. It is believed, Aretha said, her Soul was in the lost and found, while not knowing what-to-do.

626. What's love got to do with it? Love has everything to do with it. He died for me.

627. He So Loved the world that He gave His best. This was not a second hand emotion.

628. My Soul was sinking deep within itself, while He stoop lower than low to catch me.

629. I was on my way to a Devil's Hell prepared for me.

630. Jesus Himself has a place prepared for me.

631. My Grandma said, she can do all things through Jesus, a belt and a black cup of coffee.

632. So many of us live for the moment and not for the future.

633. Many of us cannot see the future, because we are still stuck in our past.

634. We as people of color must deny our friendship with the miseries of misery.

635. Your thoughts determine your destiny.

636. As paraphrased, the Mother of a well-known Black leader once said, Son, I will meet you at the exchange counter, where I will turn in my cross for my crown.

637. It is what it is, but it is what you make it.

638. Just a person's voice has more power over words, than what words may say.

639. Your voice carry more weight than your prayers; the Lord knows His own.

640. We must learn to shed that same Grace and Mercy aboard.

641. My darkness and God's light are the same. What a Mighty God we serve.

642. What the shadow does is cast darkness upon God's People.

643. Be sure, your Sin will find you out. Regardless to whatever may be your logic.

644. My children insist that I love one more, than I love the other.

645. One says, I treat the other one like a baby.

646. The other says, I did more for the others than her.

647. The other says, I love him more than her.

648. Ain't the Lord good?

649. Folks will count you dead and eulogized, while you are still alive.

650. We slipped into this world and we can surely slip out without a warning notice.

651. Mine me, it shall be that somebody else will remove our shoes in a dying hour.

652. Nobody likes the valley experience. Yet, it may be the most undesirable, but the best.

653. The valley has moist and fertile soil with green grass; your Blessing awaits you in the valley.

654. Lots of us have already been where we are going.

655. Lots of us are going where we have already been.

656. If we ain't careful the church will suffer for a lack of knowledge and understanding.

657. Momma use to say, come here boy and let me give you a dose of medicine.

658. Her dose was castor oil with a piece of cornbread and syrup.

659. Favor is God's currency for our best benefit.

660. His currency is better than our clamoring currency.

661. Take authority now.

662. Live with overflow in your life. Just enough is never enough.

663. The best part of waking up is *"soldiers"* in your cup. This was stated by the little boy.

664. The best part of waking up is not soldiers, but coffee in your cup and a mind stayed on Jesus.

665. We must learn to live a fasted life. A life which requires the best behavior before the Lord.

666. The valley experiences always come unannounced.

667. David found himself in the valley, which was not his intent.

668. There are times, which we stumble and step all over ourselves.

669. The valley of the shadow of death; not death itself, but an

intimidating shadow.

670. Any shadow creates fret, hopelessness; feelings of being lost, while making one timid.

671. The Lord knows how to mix the bad with the good for our good.

672. He is good to the last drop.

673. Why is it that...when traffic moves slows at 5pm, we call it the rush hour?

674. Why do we park on a driveway and drive on a parkway?

675. Why do women wear lip stick, but their lips still continuously move all the time?

676. Why do we entrust our hard earned money to brokers?

677. The mortality rate is lower for those consistently attending church.

678. Never answer your cellphone while in the Worship, unless it's the Lord calling.

679. The DNA of righteousness has not been scientifically studied.

680. Never speak against yourself, because *"against"* walks

and stays with you wherever.

681. Animals created to look down; man was made to look up.

682. We have a habit of looking at *"NNN"* and following after *"Furry Foxxes;"* look unto the Lord.

683. Never use your stress voice. Even Siri does not know a stressed voice. Be not anxious.

684. Man has demonstrated over and over that he does not know what to do.

685. Science disproves man, but proves God.

686. Sometimes, we build where we should have farmed.

687. The edge of night is where darkness refuses to let day-break.

688. It's amazing what you can see, when you decide not to look at the forbidden.

689. The darkest is not all bad; just feel your way through any-how.

690. Lots of times, we tell our minds what's not there, instead of what's there.

691. If we allow, change will start in our valley experiences.

692. When you think you rule, you are actually ruining.

693. The church of today has missed her calling.

694. Hold on, a change is coming.

695. Help me, help you to help me.

696. By the way, leave the light on for the Baby Jesus.

697. The *"Saviour"* came as a Blessing, not a handout.

698. In all states, you are in good hands.

699. This world is fading away.

700. Speak to your own storm; make it obey and be still.

701. We must learn to get up off our do nothings and do something.

702. You can pray, until you faint, unless you get up off your do nothings.

703. Faith without works is dead and needs a burial.

704. Sometimes, we burn the candle at both ends.

705. You had better keep your eye on the middle, lest you have a meltdown.

706. Life begins before conception. Jeremiah says...I knew you, before I formed you.

707. We must give God a reason to answer our prayer.

708. The Black Church is becoming a SLEEPING GIANT in the midst of a lost people.

709. We Believe in the His Virgin birth. We Believe in His dying on the cross...

710. Yet, we fail to Believe Him for everything in between His birth and death.

711. Unbelief is an obstruction to your Faith.

712. Lord, I Believe, but help me with my unbelief.

713. We must map out our successes with a plan.

714. Failing to plan is planning to fail.

715. We are born with the odds against us. With God, we can do all things.

716. Don't beg for what you do not need.

717. Be careful about what you ask for...you just might get it and the burden too.

718. God's Favor is all over you.

719. You must announce and pronounce your Blessings into reality; speak it into the air.

720. Speak an affirmation and confirmation too.

721. Ain't know hurt like church hurt.

722. Church hurt supersedes loss of a job, divorce and even death.

723. Momma used to say, live and let live.

724. Never put the pastor out to pasture.

725. There are times, when we are betwixt a rock and a hard place.

726. There are three ways, which we can take a loss in this life.

727. All losses either come through kinship, friendship and ownership. Just ask Job about his losses.

728. The hardest part of going through is finding yourself.

729. We are not of our own. Naked came I into the world; naked shall I return.

730. The Devil went down to Georgia by Charlie Daniels.

731. We are sometimes picked out to be picked on.

732. One thing about a lie; it does not care who tells it.

733. If you are a garbage can, people will keep bringing you garbage.

734. Next, you will be the **BIG** green dumpster.

735. Fight for what you want, if not...what you don't want will take over.

736. Fight the fight with good Faith.

737. **GET READY! GET READY!** And **GET READY!** Even the more.

738. Momma use to say, *"You are slower than pond water."*

739. Also, she would say, you can't pour pee out of a boot, boy.

740. Also, she said, laziness will kill you, boy.

741. Likewise, her words to me were, *"I CAN'T, he, die a long time ago."*

742. Never say, I CAN'T around Momma, unless you meant it for sure. Might get your butt whipped.

743. Momma would eat your lunch up, if you used the cliché, "*I thought.*"

744. Never tell Momma, "*I meant to.*" She will eat your lunch up.

745. I am a firm believer, she could beat the Devil out of you with a plaited switch.

746. That fanny would be tore up; all foolishness ceased.

747. The visibility of her switch kept law and order, while ruling from the corner post of the house.

748. Never let a situation change you; you change the situation.

749. Waiting on things to change? You change.

750. Waiting on things to get better? You get better.

751. During your wait, celebrate.

752. We are success in progress.

753. Lean on the everlasting arms; His arms won't ever give away.

754. Even the baby trust a Mother's arms when sleeping.

755. We ought to try sleeping in the Arms of the Lord, instead

of fretting.

756. "It don't get no "*gooder*," than that...Uttered words from a self-proclaimed White person.

757. While in class, this Black student said, he was going to go drop a bomb.

758. In Black language, that's equivalent to taking a dump.

759. In Black language, that means going to the bathroom.

760. In a White translation, that means to drop an actual bomb.

761. The White interpretation means a student with felony charges.

762. Well, such incident happened. The big social divide, because of culture differences.

763. Black housing projects change names, but kept the same social problems.

764. A name change for a Black housing project does not change social problems.

765. A name change means, no improvements for safety and health of the facilities.

766. Be careful. It ain't always fight or flight.

767. Black Lives seems to have no matter.

768. A giving God. Why can't we take His lead and be not so nitty?

769. Population reduction started back, when Herod the Great slaughtered all boy babies.

770. The war on drugs is categorized as a war on people of color.

771. Remember, the Lord keeps a master plan.

772. Bad things lead to good things. Christianity spread after the stoning of Stephen.

773. Don't get upset. Don't fret; Evil will destroy itself.

774. Not only itself, but the supporters of Evil too.

775. Look, listen and learn. The order of each day for total success.

776. Fear is contagious, so is Hope.

777. To look up and live was against the odds. Yet, Moses used a snaked cane for victory.

778. Our God is very abstract. You never know, until He shows-up and shows-out.

779. Nature lost her velocity, because her Creator was dying a death filled with agony.

780. In all things give thanks, not for the situation, but for God's hand in the situation.

781. If you don't want to miss out, you don't have to...

782. There are two different things going on; those that love and those that don't love.

783. Some have an opportunity to love, others and opportunity to seek. Do one of the two.

784. Proverbs 8:17 brings us into the arena of how to love and seek our God.

785. The one gruesome things about life is that we must deal with trials and tribulations.

786. The prodigal left a perfect world and went into an imperfect world.

787. What the prodigal had and saw everyday was perfect.

788. What he thought was perfect, was not perfect. His eyes shone an imperfect allusion, which caused him hardship with

suffering and pain.

789. Lots of times the grass is not greener on the other side.

790. Seeing too much, can fool you. Grass turns colors too.

791. Ask Abraham's Lot about grass.

792. We ought to Bless the Lord where we are at the moment.

793. Our premises are protected by Him who does not sleep nor slumber.

794. Release from prison, nobody wanted the football giant, Michael Vick.

795. Yet, somebody took him to redemption and restoration.

796. Likewise, when it seems as if nobody wants you, remember somebody wants you.

797. The Lord redeems and then restores. Just ask the prodigal.

798. There is somebody for everybody.

799. Jesus is somebody for everybody.

800. Hold on, hold onto your "*holt*," help is on the way.

801. There is a difference in leading a flock and herding a flock.

802. Lord, at your feet... I am too far away. Lord, at your foot... I am closer.

803. In the sight of God, you are the head and not the tail.

804. Whose report are you going to believe? The prognosis of Satan or the diagnosis of Jesus?

805. Your life and your death is within the power of your tongue. Live or die, your choice.

806. Quit hitting the replay button in your life.

807. Live and let live requires us to give, take and make do with others.

808. It is believed, Dr. Clay Evans said, you may be White or you may be Black, all are precious in His sight.

809. We all are more alike than not alike; the same Creator; the same Maker.

810. There was a time, when all we had were a radio and no television in the house.

811. Now, the Old Saintly Women are saying, "Child, I got WIFI in my house." So funny...

812. If you go wireless, make sure you stay connected to Jesus.

813. Death disproves mankind, but after the Resurrection, Jesus approves mankind.

814. We must learn to look past the natural and see the spiritual.

815. Jesus is not our ticket to bypass Hell, but our ticket to Heaven.

816. The Lord is a right now God for a right now people.

817. Sin has a concealed boomer rang, designed to find you out.

818. Are there days when you have to itch and can't scratch?

819. Ask the Lord to lead and keep you, where you need to be led and kept.

820. We are living in trying times, where the Word of God seems to be a menace to mankind.

821. The world is reeling and rocking; mankind has grown to become destructive towards creation.

822. If you will let Ole Man Wisdom have his perfect way, your way will become plain and prosperous.

823. Never raise holy hell. Live and let live, until Heaven speaks down from Eternity.

824. Lord block the ugly out of my life that beauty may shine forth as glistening light.

825. People do hard things, say hard things.

826. While in the valley, look up at the right mountain; all your help comes from above.

827. Evil has become an intruding rodent within our society. It ain't black, ain't white; it's Evil.

828. My skin color has been interrogated so many times, till it's exhausting for my Blackness.

829. Every day of my life, I show the way; not ask the way.

830. Jesus always shows the way, because He is the Way. He never stops to ask directions.

831. Life comes and goes without fringe benefits, unless you have been saved by the Blood.

832. It's a good day for a good day. All depends upon you.

833. This era has caused our beings and spirits to have been transfused from us.

834. Speak life and power into existence by the authority which has been granted you.

835. What use to be right has become wrong; what use to be wrong has become right.

836. Moses left and went into the mountains; Martin King left and went into the mountains too.

837. Well, who *"is"* you? Not who are you, but who *"is"* you? Find your mountain and go.

838. Our society has retooled everything. Now, two plus two equals, twenty-two.

839. Our society has created a tool of vengeance; snitches get stiches.

840. Our society has spun into a *"raggin"* drunk.

841. Sin has great taste, but less filling.

842. Sin is a payday loan that's hard to payback.

843. When we pray, our bodies ventilate.

844. This world has gone to Hell in a handbasket.

845. Life is a good teacher of things.

846. Life as we once knew it...is gradually dissipating from humanity.

847. Mortality has taken its toll on creation and the worth of humanity.

848. God's Sovereignty has been smothered a bit by the Sin nature of man.

849. God's Goodness goes hand-in-hand with our Faithfulness.

850. Don't pretend your Faith, be your Faith.

851. Not only be your Faith, but wear your Faith.

852. Wish there were more Carl Winslow Daddies of Color.

853. Maybe you need a Steve Urkel in your life, right now.

854. Lord, don't let my external get into my internal.

855. A watchful subordinate to His crucifixion said, "*Surely this must have been the Son of God.*"

856. He is Lord Almighty and by default, we are somebody.

857. We should have at least five goals for each day.

858. Daily living with purpose will build the contents of our character.

859. Everybody plays the fool; no exceptions to the rule.

860. It may be factual; it may be cruel; but you can become the fool.

861. You can talk yourself out of something; the same time talking yourself into something.

862. If you think too long, you have already gone wrong.

863. Your attitude determines your altitude and how high you can climb.

864. Blessings come in the waiting. Try waiting every now and then.

865. I am shaking my tree, because every good and perfect gift comes from above.

866. There must be three hedges in your life. One around you, one around your family and one around your possessions.

867. Satan looks for your hedges and the height of each hedge.

868. The first legal case was recorded in the Gospel of John, Chapter Eight.

869. Mayhem is the one that sits on your roof plotting the next incident.

870. Mayhem is the one that makes your cellphone fall on the floor while you driving.

871. Mayhem is the one that ruins weddings.

872. Mayhem does other stuff too.

873. By-the-way, Clifford the Big Red Dog is the only BIG DOG around; not you.

874. What is the difference in the words provision and provider?

875. Jesus is both the provision and provider of the provision.

876. Too mean to live, unfit to die. Is that you?

877. The old deacon said, he was too mean to live; unfit to die on his way to a Devil's Hell.

878. Unfit means, your house ain't in order for the reckoning with death.

879. It is believed, Bob Dylan gave his Soul to the Devil in exchange for his popularity and success.

880. A lie will not hold water long enough.

881. It takes a lie to support a lie.

882. Taught sense is better than bought sense.

883. Why buy bought sense by being incarcerated in prison; the price is too high.

884. Sometimes, it hard to get the head and heart aligned together.

885. Life is like a roll of toilet paper; the closer it gets to the end, the faster it goes.

886. When opportunity and preparation collide, Blessings come.

887. Job said, in my flesh, I shall see God.

888. *"It's not what you gather, but it's what you scatter"*. (Sam Walton's Wife)

889. Sin has a way of duping us, while leaving us holding the bag.

890. Some folks think they are big, but little got them.

891. Pride is like bad breath; everybody knows it, except you.

892. The church is filled with whiners; not drunkards.

893. Looking at the negative, but living in the positive.

894. We were born, not to fit in, but stand out.

895. You can't evangelize and antagonize at the same time. Leave one at home somewhere.

896. Martin King did not stand down, but stood up.

897. Who is doing the most drawing in your life? You or the Lord?

898. Both the Lord and the Devil are working at the same time. One against another.

899. Some went, some sent and some were called.

900. In some places, street preaching is a breach of peace. Times are changing, when it comes to the Gospel presentation of Christ.

901. Where were you when my son died? These were the anguishing words of a Mother to the Lord in her prayers. The Lord replied, the same place, I was when my Son died.

902. Always, give time... some more time.

903. Learn how to fall forward; not backwards.

904. Another one bites the dust.

905. Time will always side against you, if you don't grab its ad-

vantages.

906. Our life is the sum results of our choices.

907. Be a Blessing and not a turkey.

908. If you think your parents are tough, wait until you get a boss.

909. Flipping burgers is nothing, but an opportunity.

910. Despise not small beginnings.

911. Opportunity come to the optimistic, not the pessimistic.

912. Never Believe that Evil will outweigh good.

913. Be nice to nerds. Chances are... one day, they will become your boss on the job.

914. Expect excellence in all things done.

915. Your attitude seems little, but makes a big difference.

916. Get caught reading and studying.

917. Once you discover your limits exceed them.

918. STRANGER DANGER; watch out.

919. Readers do make leaders.

920. Sin will take you little further than what was intended.

921. A second to get into, years to get out of...

922. We all shall not sleep, but we shall be caught up in the air to meet Him.

923. The universe says, yes to whatever you say, ask, or do.

924. Watch what you say. The universe acts on what's said and heard; good or bad.

925. The little boy said, Momma, I see his *"teefies"* laughing at me.

926. Unlike pencils, some mistakes don't have erasers on top.

927. You can't find it, if it ain't meant for you to find.

928. The secret to growing old is to avoid dying at all cost.

929. Unlike the lost sheep. One lady said, she had ninety-nine bobby pins and can't find one.

930. Share your light and others will find their way.

931. Have confidence in nothing, but always staying on your knees before the Lord.

932. Times have changed, but the roads to righteous are the same.

933. It takes effort to do right.

934. Never do for others, what they can do for themselves.

935. God is the head of man.

936. Man is the head of the woman.

937. Woman is the head of the children.

938. The children are over the dog.

939. Evil has a pervasive gesture in our society as we now know it.

940. The Lord knows a man's heart and the intents of his heart.

941. Wherever and whenever Evil can lurk, it lurks.

942. Evil lurks in the eye of your fridge, television and even cellphone.

943. Evil is a spy; Evil tends to erupt and expose good.

944. Evil virtually hates good at our expense.

945. This old usher shouted from the back of the church.... *"TANK YOU LORD! TANK YOU!"*

946. We have not, because we ask not.

947. This is the main problem in our lives. We have not ask.

948. Many of us live half-hearted lives of what will be an attitude of carelessness.

949. I beg the difference. What will be, will be, because of what you allow it to become.

950. Safety is of the Lord, Himself.

951. We have no ability to keep ourselves.

952. When it comes to people of color, our lives have already been mapped out.

953. Life never balances itself out; rich here; poor there.

954. Poor here; can be rich there.

955. A pastor stated, that he can never get life balanced, no matter how hard he tries.

956. When the church is happy and job is okay, the wife and children have gone crazy.

957. When the job, wife and children are okay, the church is in an uproar.

958. When the church, wife and children are happy and okay, then the job is off the chain.

959. We are constantly putting out fires in this life.

960. I tell folks, I am the first responder for my own fires.

961. When we say thank you to others, we actually feeding good into the Spirit of our Souls.

962. Many of us are sitting on a gold mine, not digging deep enough for the gold.

963. Some of us are living on borrowed time; the time which was disallowed to others.

964. Satan is a bad boy, but our God is a good God.

965. Folks talk about Satan being busy; no, he is Evil.

966. Satan does not want to make you mad, he wants to take you out.

967. The butler forgot Joseph, but God's Grace did not forget Joseph.

968. The Old folk used to say, Mercy suits all my cases.

969. When the doctor says no, remember who can say, yes.

970. A drug user in prison thirteen months, two days, and two hours confessed God's Grace.

971. The drug user said, our God is a God of second chances for everyone.

972. Early is on time, on time is late and late is unacceptable.

973. We are pencils, which have come to be sharpened by the Lord.

974. Madera said, it ain't what people call you, but it's what you answer to when called.

975. Taking a stand by keeping your seat. Thank you, Ms. Rosa for showing us the way.

976. Good things come to those who wait; not to those who wait too late.

977. Wait with anticipation.

978. It's Faithless to wait without anticipation of anything happening.

979. The secret of waiting for God is waiting on God without seeing Him.

980. God smiled on me.

981. Most people want to be, but don't want to do, to become.

982. Being on God's side, not Him on your side is very wise thinking.

983. He is our pilot, not co-pilot.

984. We serve a God of many languages, yet of one voice.

985. There is a place in Heaven for me when the toils of this life are over.

986. Hell has a way of making our lives bitter, but Heaven endears our lives.

987. The old folks would say, the Lord has got an angel keeping watch over their heart beat by *"nite."*

988. It ain't your sight, but your vision.

989. It's where you want to go and what you want to do.

990. Prayer still works, it brings you up and out.

991. Up and out of the muck and mire.

992. *"Tough Love"* makes a real man and a Blessed woman.

993. We are in enemy territory, while passing through on this side of what is known as life.

994. It's getting ready to get better.

995. Take them to the Lord and leave them there.

996. God's Grace will stay as close as you allow.

997. Apparently, our problem is with asking the Lord.

998. Sin will upset the status quo.

999. Read the leaflets in your Bible; there might be paper money stuffed between them.

1000. This Mother sent her son off to college. He kept complaining about not having money.

1001. The Mother kept saying the same thing over and over. Read your Bible, son.

1002. The Lord is saying the same thing over and over to us. Read your Bible, sons and daughters.

1003. Do what you are *"pose"* to do. *"Git"* what you are *"pose"* to have.

1004. Is there stuff in your gulf?

1005. *"Mize"* well *"git"* ready, we all have *"pointment"* with death.

1006. Big Momma would say, look at God work.

1007. There are times when your Goodness is taken for weakness.

1008. When I am weak, I am strong.

1009. Sometimes life can be a hellish fiasco.

1010. Shiftless people distrust God.

1011. God can read lips, minds, hearts and tears.

1012. Sometimes, we find ourselves in bully situations.

1013. All is well with me

1014. The Old Folk would say, if I had ten thousand tongues, I could not praise Him enough.

1015. Pastors go thru so much and very few say, thank you.

1016. By now, he *"stinketh"* in the grave.

1017. Unless you have been there, you don't know.

1018. Unless you have worn my shoes, you don't know.

1019. Some Believers need corrective lens.

1020. Some Believers have blurred vision.

1021. Some Believers need cataracts removed.

1022. Some Believers are just blind and can't see.

1023. Yet, that's why they don't see the mote in their own eyes.

1024. What to do, when you don't know what to do.

1025. Ask the Lord to besiege you with His Army.

1026. Amazing sight the *"Saviour Stands"* at every door and knocks.

1027. A man stands mighty tall when he stoops to help a child.

1028. On our knees bring us into eye level with a child.

1029. Hell at midnight is the hardest hour to live through.

1030. This was the case of Jesus meeting the cross on death's terms.

1031. A Believer's itinerary includes trials and tribulations.

1032. The case of the *"I can't help its."* Who has it?

1033. Lots of times, enticements come from what you can't see.

1034. Blind Bartimaeus had a vision; his vision was to see.

1035. We can see, but have no vision in sight.

1036. Release the seed and receive the harvest.

1037. There are somethings only the Lord knows.

1038. Peter talked a lots; talk is cheap. Ask Peter, He knows best.

1039. The best gift ever wrapped was Jesus.

1040. You may think the Lord is going to do it this way and He does it that way.

1041. Your integrity will see you through.

1042. Imitate good and good will follow good.

1043. There is good everywhere; just find it and do it.

1044. Always go after good, even when wrong hurts you.

1045. Momma told me everything *"gonna"* be alright.

1046. Jesus told me everything *"gonna"* be alright. Alright; Alright.

1047. His power has been a major fascination to people of color.

1048. When you don't understand which direction God is coming from, just try looking up.

1049. Our thoughts, our words, and deeds create our reality.

1050. He giveth, He taketh away.

1051. Don't be a butt, but go after it.

1052. Opportunity comes to those who look for it.

1053. It's hard to live, but easy to die.

1054. To ask is to know.

1055. Embrace change like a new friend.

1056. Opportunity might come twice; use it or lose it.

1057. You may be without, but not alone.

1058. Whatever the mind conceives can be achieved.

1059. Life scars leave plenty of reminders which are hard to forget.

1060. Living in the hood will drive us to pray; even the more.

1061. God and one other is the majority; the majority rules.

1062. PUSH and PRAY, until something happens

1063. Faith grows as a person climbs higher and higher.

1064. The more you know, the farther you go.

1065. Our word is no longer our bond in these days and times.

1066. The 2020 COVID-19 has redefined the handshake.

1067. Social distancing ain't just started, since COVID. We were already hitting and missing in church on Sundays.

1068. The people that complain the most are the ones that ain't *"gonna"* to do nothing.

1069. Our destiny is at stake, when we underestimate or over-estimate life.

1070. Is prayer your steering wheel or your spare wheel?

1071. Some of us use prayer for a First Aid Kit and Jesus for an impromptu second responder.

1072. He is Master of the Sea in my disparity.

1073. Prepare for the worst and pray for the best.

1074. God is up to something when you are down to nothing.

1075. Ain't no dangers in God's Water.

1076. Make a pause for the cause.

1077. A most definite, people of color are stricken with hardships on every hand.

1078. That's why the preacher must lift words off the pages and plant them into the hearts of waiting Souls.

1079. God's Word will find you where you are and put you on another page.

1080. It is believed, Gladys Knight said, *"I rather live with him in his world, than live without him in my world."*

1081. The same can be said of the Lord.

1082. Follow your compass, not your clock.

1083. Trusting God means having an ironing board for the kitchen table.

1084. Trusting God means eating a mayonnaise sandwich, when you ain't got nothing else.

1085. Trusting God means eating a ketchup sandwich to killed a hunger.

1086. Trusting God means eating *"Roman"* Noodles breakfast and dinner.

1087. In the Hood, we say, *"Roman"* noodles.

1088. Noodles and Faith in Jesus will take you all the way through college and bring you out.

1089. *"Shout in church; march in the picket lines."* (Pastor Jeremiah Wright, Chicago)

1090. What would the Black Experience be like without a Martin Luther King, Jr.?

1091. Wasted time see things as they are and not as they ought to be.

1092. Be kind today, because tomorrow might not come.

1093. When you do for others, you are doing for yourself.

1094. Go higher with the Lord and the rainbow will show itself to you; just for you.

1095. The child Mary came to deliver, delivered us.

1096. Anything worth having is worth working for...that your Soul can rest well at night.

1097. Somebody said, I was down, but He did not leave me down.

1098. Let your mind do the walking through the yellow pages.

1099. I am almost to the point; I can call the Lord by His first name.

1100. Jesus is His first name; the Christ is His title.

1101. *"Let His Blood be on us and our children."* Life and death is in the power of the tongue.

1102. The three boys, including the bad Negro experienced the heat being up and the temperature down.

1103. HEAT UP, TEMPERATURE DOWN. His Power to be reckon *"wit"* in the fiery furnace.

1104. This day and time, people are taking on death blindly than taking Eternal life openly.

1105. Lord look at my oversights; we prayer for insight, foresight and hindsight.

1106. When people finally realize what you have done, you have already done it.

1107. We must learn to win from within.

1108. Win any struggle from within.

1109. Words have the exact power which we put in them.

1110. Never let failure come into your mind.

1111. Go back and find the old path and walk there-in.

1112. Some of us are willing to settle for anything; I do not want to be the tail of anything.

1113. Tail of the bus, tail of the line, tail of the plane, because the tail has to follow.

1114. When you are the head, you can see where you are headed.

1115. His Grace gives defense, when my Skin Color can't defend my case.

1116. There is a leak in this *"Ole Body"* and my Soul has got to move.

1117. People are like refrigerators, we can't keep nothing.

1118. Never assume your steps; you are subject to a misstep.

1119. A good man places his steps into the footstep imprints of

God.

1120. We fall down, but we get up.

1121. A man without a future, constantly looks back to the past.

1122. You never know how good your good is...until your good is gone.

1123. Life is frail and fragile.

1124. I have been told, whether you are going to Heaven or Hell, you will go by way of Atlanta for your connection.

1125. You will not be late for this flight.

1126. This flight will have an on time departure.

1127. This flight will make the right connections.

1128. This flight will makes the right landing.

1129. Walk in His way; stay in His way.

1130. Tread light wherever your feet go.

1131. Don't sweat the small stuff.

1132. There is a difference in measuring the height verses the length; don't miss the obvious.

1133. Life can go either way.

1134. Don't pawn your future hopes.

1135. The Ole Saints would say, "*I have come too far to turn around now.*"

1136. God don't like ugly, no matter how beautiful it looks.

1137. Make yourself mean something to yourself, regardless of what others think of "*you.*"

1138. Slow down a minute and catch up.

1139. Slow down and let yourself catch up with the real you.

1140. Avoid letting your Soul separate from you.

1141. Our bodies are decaying; the Bible call them earthly tabernacles.

1142. The Black Experience for blended children carries its own cares and concerns.

1143. Are you the one or is there another?

1144. What do you do when someone steps in your corn flakes?

1145. There are times when our money starts acting funny. Is your change acting strange too?

1146. A comma before the word *"but"* negates everything that was previously stated.

1147. Living on automatic is a dangerous disadvantage; failure to first consult the Lord leads to destruction.

1148. Some of us are running and nobody is chasing us.

1149. Sooner or later, death will serve a warrant on each of us.

1150. Excuses are for the people that make them; nobody else needs an excuse.

1151. Meekness is power in control.

1152. You do you, and I do me.

1153. I want to be like Old Man Job, with the suffering; coming out smelling like a rose.

1154. Life is sometimes a few French Fries short of a Happy Meal.

1155. A married couple are two hearts and one beat.

1156. Some of us are digging our own grave and preaching our own eulogy.

1157. Don't settle for crumbs.

1158. The Old Folk in the midst of an argument saying, it's the "*God Heaven knows truth.*"

1159. The psalmist said, I cried and the Lord heard me; saved me from all my fears.

1160. Trust in God, can't be taught, but it is best learned.

1161. The Devil is in the mix. Devil's food cake mix.

1162. God is not a fair God, but He is a Just God.

1163. When it feels like the worst, it's really becoming the best.

1164. Many times, we think the Lord has mismanaged our situation, but he has not.

1165. He is too wise to make a mistake.

1166. He is routing us to our destiny with a waiting Blessing.

1167. Job was Blessed even the more at the latter end than the beginning.

1168. Ain't the Lord good; all the time the Lord is good, even when a Soul floods.

1169. Satan wants your demise, so that he can give your demise over to a pending death.

1170. In return, death gives your Soul back to Satan for culling; to determine, if you meet the criteria for Heaven or Hell.

1171. Sickness, dying and death are warm allies; they have a way of sharing personal warmth.

1172. It behooves us to know the real enemy death. He does all to snuff us out without notice.

1173. I have seen him interrupt prayer services with talking Demons launching out in the pews.

1174. I have seen my Carolina Elders slaughtered by evilness, while in prayer meeting.

1175. I have seen coffee splatter all over the place by itself, after a violence move of prayer services.

1176. For many of us, we will outlive our dream.

1177. Likewise, for many of us, our dream will outlive us.

1178. We have no comprehension of God's Will for us.

1179. We should pray...if it be your Will Lord, this or that...

1180. The Book of Job is not about the mystery of suffering.

1181. The Book of Job is about the mystery of God and His movements.

1182. The Gospel of Jesus has many life giving streams which to quench thirst.

1183. Life is not to be feared, but understood.

1184. The end ain't yet.

1185. A New Normal has become reality.

1186. Society has become inconsistent and unpredictable for the survival of mankind.

1187. We had better hold on to the Lord's unchanging hands; society as once known, will be no more.

1188. The New World System has confiscated our old world system; to include our livelihood.

1189. Jesus will soon make a grand entrance for His waiting Church, without spot or wrinkle.

1190. The mind is the matrix of all matter.

1191. Hell is seven times hotter than scalding grits, without margarine.

1192. Seven is the total completion of things to come.

1193. A nonconscious mind will lead the body anywhere.

1194. A conscious mind cooperates whether it's right or wrong; it obeys good and bad.

1195. A subconscious mind will think for you and keep life, provided you let it take care of you.

1196. Death is precious when you are a Believer in Christ Jesus.

1197. Why don't you fellowship with the Lord, by dunking Graham Crackers in milk today.

1198. Sop with Him and He with you.

1199. God does how He wants, what He wants, to whom He wants, when He wants, Where He wants.

1200. What's you beef?

1201. Take it for what it's worth; avoid shacking together.

1202. Praying in the past tense, means it has already come and happened.

1203. Serving the Lord don't pay a whole lots, but the benefits are out of this world.

1204. The Lord pays hazardous duty pay. Ask Ole Man Job

about his bonus pay.

1205. Some of us have it made for life, but we throw our lives away to the dogs.

1206. Everybody wants to go Heaven, but nobody wants to die, nor fly.

1207. Everybody wants Salvation, but nobody wants to be saved.

1208. What we need, we don't want.

1209. What we want, we don't need.

1210. What we desire, we don't ask.

1211. What to do, when you don't know what to do.

1212. The things we deal with in the church house are pure Evil.

1213. The Devil wears all kinds of uniforms. Be careful, he just might be your delivery man.

1214. He came to the front of an elderly lady's house posed as a merchantman, but he was actually attempting to serve a death notice. She recanted to opening the door for the merchantman.

1215. Be careful, he just might be your befriended one.

1216. Sometimes the Lord wants to know, if He has anything in your life to work with.

1217. Jesus is not a subordinate to God. Whatever Jesus does, God does it too.

1218. Thank God for what was, even though it's now gone.

1219. Job says, He gives and He takes away.

1220. There are times when you and I put ourselves on trial, because of the weakness of our Faith.

1221. We preoccupy ourselves with crying instead of praying and making acclamation.

1222. I have no idea why, we have to drink tears for water.

1223. The things of this world are foolish compared to what has been prepared in Heaven.

1224. Weeping does not make us any less of a person. "*Jesus wept.*"

1225. We can live large in lean times without all the cuts. The Lord is all sufficient in lean times.

1226. Even the Devil goes to church on Sunday mornings.

1227. Where the ghetto meets the Hood.

1228. Our trials are under the management of God.

1229. Lay with dogs, get fleas.

1230. Never except your world as it is, but as you want it.

1231. There are times when we are driven to our knees, when we have nowhere else to go.

1232. Trials and tribulations can be the most defining moment of life.

1233. Check to see, if you have a dark spot in your life. Satan is looking for that same spot too.

1234. The harder it gets, the harder we must pray.

1235. Some of us ain't living unless, we find a problem to drag along.

1236. Peter did not know the difference in an invitation verses a command.

1237. Learn from some things and run from somethings.

1238. Seeing everything, but not paying attention to anything; this is today's quick society.

1239. All of my life as a child, I always looked for a person named Charles to walk through the church doors during devotion. Why?

1240. The old deacons sung, *"Hey Charles to Keep a God to Glorify"*.

1241. This Black Mother talked about Job so much, till her daughter thought Job was her first cousin.

1242. Live fast, die sooner and forgettable quicker.

1243. Until you run out of excuses, you can't fully trust God for the end results.

1244. There set a recycle bin labeled Colored Paper. Well, where is the label for the other bin?

1245. Ain't politically correct to say, do you have any white out? Now it's called correction ink.

1246. Ain't politically correct to say, do you have a staple gun? Now, we say, stapler.

1247. Ain't politically correct to have a yard stick in your hand at the school house; a symbol of creating student intimidation.

1248. Now, you know why students can't tell a foot from a yard.

1249. Daddy would say Son, time brings about a change.

1250. A White man can teach me how to be wealthy, but I can teach him on making ends meet in the village.

1251. Church in the neighborhood consist of locked doors during the tithes and offering time.

1252. Shape up before you ship out.

1253. The Black Church has fat shepherds for pastors and plenty skinny sheep for members.

1254. Any man that stays on his knees before God, can stand before any man and situation.

1255. In hard times, God only provides just enough to make it.

1256. I wonder, why?

1257. Doors closed, doors opened.

1258. As long as we are in this world, we are not the finished product.

1259. Knowing what to overlook makes a person wise.

1260. When troubles lurks, contain your mind.

1261. Church Praise and Worship is considered spiritual aerobics for the healing of the Soul.

1262. Never fear the known. Keep your eye on the unknown.

1263. Two marks of a Christian are his or her giving and for-giving.

1264. Remember, eggs cannot be unscrambled.

1265. Eggs shells cannot be glued back when cracked.

1266. Arrive Alive.

1267. Be careful, other folks will talk you out of your dream.

1268. I heard two women talking another woman out of her marriage.

1269. You are your own enemy; know yourself.

1270. Avoid social media. It will haunted you when least ex-pected.

1271. Social media is like casting your bread upon the waters and in many days, it may return to eat your butt.

1272. Your death bed will remind you of what was not done and what should have been done.

1273. If you fail to make your own day, somebody else will

make your day for you.

1274. There are only so many more tomorrows.

1275. All of us are running out of tomorrows, after each day we live.

1276. We will never know; today may be our last day.

1277. If you are going through Hell, don't stop, keep going; *"git"* out of there with haste.

1278. No looking back either.

1279. The Lord brought Shadrach, Meshach, and the bad Negro out of a hot fiery furnace.

1280. Think outside the box. Today drink your coffee in a Mason jar without sugar and cream.

1281. The Spirit of Excellence is a habit that can't be broken; just a way of life.

1282. Avoid waking up like an accident that just happened. There may not be enough make-up to put on your face.

1283. It's a bad thing to be lost and nobody looking for a Sin Sick you.

1284. Stay in the state of Abiding Grace. Show the brightness of your headlights, not the dimness of your tail lights.

1285. My Momma use to say, who wants to see your rusty Black butt?

1286. There is Grace, even in the state of death. It depends to whom you belong.

1287. The cost of Sin is heavy. Others will have to bear the burden of your Sin too.

1288. It hurts and pain to hear of nooses being displayed.

1289. Avoid judging others by your assessment.

1290. Out of time, there is a time.

1291. A MOST PROFOUND TEXT: And they heard the voice of the Lord God walking.

1292. How can you hear the voice of someone walking?

1293. You can be hungry, but not hungry, all at the same time; just keep living.

1294. I found my rudder stabilizer to be Jesus the Christ.

1295. "*Go and Sin no more*", suggest Sin brought on the concerned issue.

1296. Sometimes Satan can come into your thinking, if you think too long.

1297. Long brings on wrong.

1298. Long brings on suicide.

1299. Praise is a disguised warfare tool to defeat the enemy.

1300. If ants can work together, why can't we?

1301. Do couples lie about money? What is your answer?

1302. The way one knows he or she is operating in the flesh, everything has to be their way.

1303. God always looks out for little children and fools.

1304. Noah did not need flood insurance. He was assured, not insured.

1305. "*White fear means more than Black life.*" (Leonard Pitts, Miami Herald)

1306. Satan is like a devilish fly; you can't get rid of him.

1307. Never let Satan be the Master of Ceremony for your program. He will take over.

1308. There is a God-Given Divine mandate upon each of our lives.

1309. *"Waking up every day, sometimes gets you down."* (Gladys Knight)

1310. Sooner than later, we all will have a *"Garden of Gethsemane"* experience.

1311. Sweat like drops of blood will run down as we pray in agony.

1312. God always makes a way. Our job is to find the way, even when He is making it.

1313. The watchful care of a watchful God is all we need in these uncertain times.

1314. A miracle can come out of a mess.

1315. Momma would say, *"you old lying rascal."*

1316. Daddy would call a lying man a *"SamBooger."* Here comes that Ole Sambooger.

1317. If you are hiding behind a burning bush, the Lord knows, who you are and your name.

1318. Some of us need training shoes in order to follow the Lord through the green pastures.

1319. When the rabbit got the gun. The fingers you pointed are pointed back.

1320. OMG. That's when your reality become real.

1321. Stink, stank, *"stunk;"* Sin always gives off a scent.

1322. Sin leaves a paper trail to permanent exposure of the Sin and the Sinner.

1323. Nothing good comes out of devilment.

1324. Equality and Justice carry double standard meanings for people of color.

1325. Ain't no lazy bone in my butt, may get tired along the way sometimes.

1326. You can do it, put your back into.

1327. Serving God comes by way of serving others.

1328. Lack of planning does not constitute and emergency on God's part.

1329. An alarm clock is knocking on the window panes of your life.

1330. One call, that's all.

1331. It is believed, the calendar for 1986 was the same calendar for 2014.

1332. The little girl said, Nanny, where is your other face? Momma said, you have two faces anyway.

1333. Momma made me mash my **M** and **M**'s up.

1334. If Mary wrapped Him, we ought to receive Him.

1335. Black people live meager lives, yet serve a Big God; sometimes, too confusing to comprehend.

1336. The best defense is an **AWESOME** offense.

1337. Pay for what you want and beg for what you need. Bad theology.

1338. Instead of paying the electric bill, we pay the cable bill and then ask for help to pay the electric bill.

1339. It's true, you can't sit on your butt and slide uphill?

1340. God brought us, when we did not know we were being carried.

1341. Jesus paid the price, when we did not know that we were being sold.

1342. He thought, sought, caught, bought and then brought us.

1343. If you permit, you promote.

1344. The old deacon said, never give folks enough paint to paint *"wit"*...

1345. Folks will paint a big lie on the best of us, if given enough paint and colors.

1346. For every door closed, God has a window ready to pour out, which you have not enough room to receive.

1347. Clean hands and a pure heart, will get your from here to there.

1348. The Lord will meet you in Hell to see His Will done.

1349. Anytime you play games, the games are on you.

1350. Do the Do, till the Lord comes through.

1351. Fake it, till you make it. Just Do the Do, till the Lord comes through.

1352. Who in the world died and left you in charge?

1353. Wooden nickels do not spend anywhere known unto man.

1354. Looks real, but won't spend.

1355. Your work ethics will raise you above the rest.

1356. Sometimes we have to dumpster dive to make the best of a bad situation.

1357. Sometimes the good is inside the dumpster; the bad is on the outside of the dumpster.

1358. The love of many has waxed cold.

1359. Humanity is rapidly dissolving.

1360. How can a Black life be taken at the cost of selling loose cigarettes?

1361. Our definition of bad is God's definition of good. Ask the folks at the grave site of Lazarus.

1362. What we see with the eye and what God sees with His eyes are two different things.

1363. My Son said, Daddy, I want to be like other kids. My reply to him, you are not like other kids.

1364. Some of us, don't want the cat out of the bag.

1365. You can watch the footsteps of how a man walks and know his potentials.

1366. It's a good thing to be settled in your mind.

1367. It's a good thing to have a settled mind.

1368. Consider yourself as a positive living PREPOSITION; one of the most used parts of speech.

1369. Say, I am above and across.

1370. Say, I am beyond and over.

1371. Say, I am through and upon.

1372. Say, I am with... despite of.

1373. Avoid all the *"BUTS"* in your life; the *"BUTS"* negate everything you plan to do and have done.

1374. Buffet the body; subdue it. Avoid disqualifying yourself.

1375. Fasting and praying gives much authority.

1376. The New Normal is requiring much repentance from her homesteaders.

1377. Sometimes, folk will steal the glow of your countenance right-off your face.

1378. We must learn to disconnect with this world and connect with Heaven.

1379. Our prayer must be God-originated and God-initiated

for effectiveness.

1380. The Lord places a burden into our Spirit; in response, a burden for prayer originates.

1381. Once we do what is required of us, we can be heard on high.

1382. Then we can say, I besought the Lord and heard my cry; then He showed pity upon my groans.

1383. Be sick every now and then, but not unto death.

1384. Make sure you pray the Lord's *"Flavor"* into your favor.

1385. Favor ain't fair, when the Lord has flavored your favor.

1386. Sometimes, He flavors your favored flavor for His Glory and your Edification.

1387. Remember, we can never force the hand of God.

1388. Self-denial is a method of humility, which is never over-looked by the Lord.

1389. It's good not to sit at the head of the table or to be stand-ing first in-line all the time.

1390. It's most fulfilling, to live daily in the fullness of the Lord.

1391. I want my favor flavored with an anointing.

1392. I want my favor flavored with Mercy.

1393. I want mine flavored with opportunities.

1394. The beauty of a woman diminishes in a slow fade, while she ages with the years.

1395. As we travel this life, our paths do cross each other as we go along the way.

1396. Yes, prayer with an Amen does bring change with a rear-range in the midst of living.

1397. Lord, our prayer is to love you, without disgracing and shaming you.

1398. It's most confusing to watch wildlife officers give life to one hurt and dying eagle; it's even more confusing to watch peace officers take the life of one hurt and dying Black Man.

1399. A Black Man's dying body is like roadkill. The ambulance arrives lately; now late, but lately. When it arrives, it's late.

1400. Overheard a young boy saying, he was trying to get his life straight. Only the Lord can.

1401. Satan is always in the mix of things; the Lord is always in the making of things.

1402. He is in the Devil's Food mix, waiting to be baked.

1403. This life comes with a cumbersome load of care, even though the Lord knows all our sorrows.

1404. NOTE: Black suppression is REAL; don't assume "*nothin.*"

1405. Genocide is for REAL and everywhere.

1406. THE APARTHEID low-down.

1407. When you visit the toilet, just dream it, just wish it, and just do it.

1408. Just taking care of business is the order of each day.

1409. If you ever hear the ringing of a door bell in your sleep, the Lord is calling you to prayer.

1410. If you ever hear the ringing of a door bell in your sleep, the Lord is telling you something.

1411. If you ever hear the ringing of a door bell in your sleep, the Lord is telling you to watch.

1412. Never ask the Lord to give you enough, always ask Him to give you more than enough.

1413. Enough is never enough.

1414. More than enough, you will never be without according to God's standards.

1415. Never ask Him pay your bills for that week.

1416. Always, keep in mind, a new week starts on Sunday.

1417. Ask Him to pay each bill off in full.

1418. You can't be committed to anything, unless the Lord gives strength. Promises are cheap.

1419. When my table had no food, there was a knock at my front door.

1420. The Lord is more than capable; He is able.

1421. Skyping with death is a dangerous thing.

1422. The Black church at her peak is a most powerful arena in which to empower her people.

1423. Now, she is a big sleeping giant.

1424. The Lord anointed the Civil Rights Movement right out of His church at a time of her highest peak.

1425. Heavy burdens? Go to the throne, not the phone.

1426. Allow the Lord to turn you, then place you on another page at a different line.

1427. Do as Bernie Mac. Try laughing, when there ain't a whole lots to laugh about in your life.

1428. Just give it up for the Lord.

1429. *"When you don't feel like praying, that's when you ought to pray the most."* (Charles Stanley)

1430. *"We ought to be prayed up and stayed up."* (Billy Graham)

1431. Yes, sometimes our sea of despair is big, and our boat is too small. What shall I do, Lord?

1432. If you go wireless, make sure you stay connected to Jesus.

1433. Momma us to say, boy don't be long-headed. She meant, don't be a fool, *"where"* nobody can tell you anything for your own good.

1434. Perceived beauty has a way of disguising itself, until you find out what's behind the make-up and weave.

1435. Likewise, until you find out what's behind the gold grilled *"teefies,"* twenty inch rims and cologne, there is perceived beauty.

1436. Fear is contagious; so is hope too.

1437. It behooves us all to pray and spray as you go, because Jesus and germs are everywhere along the way, throughout the day.

1438. Go ahead Lord, make my day for your Glory.

1439. The bed you make is the one that you must lay-in.

1440. You made it; lay in it.

1441. Lord, hold the sting of death off; to include off kindred family and friends.

1442. Lord, sprinkle the door posts of my Soul with the Saviour's Blood.

1443. Make sure fear stays outside the door of your heart.

1444. Stay out of other folks Kool-Aid, if you don't know the flavor thereof.

1445. Never defy the odds.

1446. Small beginnings start with you; don't despise them.

1447. Let the Lord knock some sense in your head.

1448. Every now and then, when stuff shows-up, you have the right to show your true color.

1449. Some Black Folk turn from black to purple.

1450. There are two things in life which you should always defend; yourself and your cause.

1451. If need be, lay your religion down and pick it back up; then keep going in the name of the Lord.

1452. In a dispute with another, less is always more.

1453. Let them have the last word and you have the second to the last word.

1454. The rest of the story is yet to be told.

1455. What in Hell do you want?

1456. Momma would say, we never know what *"lay behead"* of us.

1457. One thing about life, never give up; press your way as the woman with the issue of blood for twelve long years.

1458. Press, until an induced change comes.

1459. If the Lord don't do it, it can't be done.

1460. Ain't no need in looking for the Five Sisters of the Three Daughters-in-law.

1461. Ain't no need in sticking needles into voodoo trolls.

1462. Some Black Folk are hampered with carrying traits of spiritual nearsightedness, due to vision limitations of the future and what it holds.

1463. Why don't you and the Lord do lunch together?

1464. If not, you and the Lord do coffee together.

1465. Faith is trying again, when all else has failed.

1466. God's ways are pass our thinking.

1467. Luck is what you were made to think.

1468. Grace is what God gives.

1469. There are no coincidences with the Lord.

1470. Believe hard enough, think hard enough, and the Lord will see you through.

1471. As the old song says, I am catching Hell.

1472. Momma would say, "*I am catching pure-T Hell.*"

1473. I beg the difference. Knowledge is not power, until it is shared.

1474. In this life, leave a little more than your last name.

1475. Papa was a rolling stone; all he left us was a bill.

1476. Leave a well-spent life with good examples to be followed.

1477. In the country our dishwater was a nasty grey. We didn't have a *"zink."*

1478. We had no rinse water. We had *"whatcha"* call dish pans for washing and rinsing.

1479. Generations ago we all drank from the same dipper. Nobody died from germs and disease.

1480. The White Man was complaining that his Black worker never shows-up on time for the job.

1481. Dearly, did he not know... Black Folk have what's called, BFT.

1482. There is Eastern, Central, Mountain, Pacific, and Black Folk Time.

1483. It seems as if time is of no essence to Black Folk.

1484. When we close our eyes under the pressure of burdens, everything goes dark.

1485. Even in the midst of burdens and darkness, Jesus can dissipate darkness into light.

1486. So you think life has you down and out. Well, have you ever seen the tears of a man while his wife is driving him to the hospital? Knowing that he may never return home again. Well, he did not...

1487. Are you the man in the mirror?

1488. This thing called life, ain't a myth, nor joke.

1489. Some of us know everything and don't know anything.

1490. Your credit score is a computerized social score which reveals the contents of your character.

1491. The checkbook, calendar and charge card statement define character contents, even the more.

1492. Every now and then say, Good Morning to yourself.

1493. When friends are far and few, invest in a stuff animal to become your main squeeze.

1494. After Blessing the food on the table, guess who's coming to dinner?

1495. The Lord will go *"behead"* of you, wherever you go; the saying of the Old Black Folk.

1496. Momma said, son, your name will go *"behead"* of you before you get there.

1497. Sometimes in life, we forfeit our Blessings, because of a lack of discreet mental insight.

1498. I have learned in life, you never know exactly which direction a lie comes from.

1499. Don't ever throw your cloak in and quit on the Lord.

1500. He is an on time God; yes He is.....

1501. Sometimes we must aerate and meditate our Spirit into the truths of God.

1502. That His Wisdom and Voice may impart into our being.

1503. There are times which we must lay prostrate before the Lord in Godly fear to be heard of Him.

1504. Whatever you desire of the Lord, broadcast it into the air and allow the wind to carry it.

1505. If the wind can carry a crazy lie, it can definitely carry our prayers to a higher dimension above the clouds.

1506. BEWARE: Whether good or bad, what goes around comes around.

1507. BEWARE: Whether good or bad, whatsoever a man "*soweth*," that shall he also reap; not almost reap, but also reap.

1508. The clock hands of Ole Man Time cannot be turned back counter clockwise.

1509. Jesus relayed to God the Father, He was content to drink from His own bitter cup of suffering and shame; the cup of His shed Blood for all mankind.

1510. How can one drink from his own bitter cup? How can one drink of Himself?

1511. So why are there such imposed radical racial variances, because of skin color, character contents, and cultural differences?

1512. Who died and left who in charge of whom? The Word says, we should be about our brother's business more than our own.

1513. Jesus Himself, died and left us in charge. He said, occupy, till I come again.

1514. We should become a Sister to Sister keeper; a Brother to Brother helper.

1515. You may never find out what makes certain people tick.

1516. A ticking person can be a dangerous person to one's safety.

1517. Stay away from FAKE NEWS, it's an illusion.

1518. There are times when the Lord wants us to be content with such as we have...

1519. *"You can always remove a staple, but the holes are permanent."* (Bria Wright, Cary North Carolina)

1520. Thirty-one percent of our teens are stressed.

1521. Saggy pants symbolizes a loss of integrity to one's content of character.

1522. Walking in the city parks can be dangerous for *"Persons of Color."*

1523. A Black Man must walk public streets with a visible described purpose; to avoid police profiling.

1524. Auntee said, us *"gonna"* make it anyhow.

1525. Avoid living to eat; eat to live.

1526. For some unknown reason, Black Folks change colors when the Lord promotes them on the job.

1527. Momma can be fussing and whipping your butt at the same time. When the phone rings in the middle of that butt beating, she calmly and politely changes her voice to no end; it sounded like nothing was ever happening.

1528. When it comes to a bad child, don't wait for the military to recruit them, you recruit the military for them.

1529. That's what you call, a skillful skillset.

1530. Lots of times, she would have you to pick your own switch from the oak tree, but it had better be the right-one.

1531. Then hang-up the phone and resume as scheduled to the previous butt whipping.

1532. Spare the rod, spoil the child; *"clare"* fore God, the truth.

1533. Had it not been for Momma, I would have been in jail or dead by now.

1534. Big Momma always said, make do *"wit"* what you got.

1535. Big Momma would say hold on to your *"holt."*

1536. Big Momma was yet holding on that we may say, we held on.

1537. This boy told his Daddy, if you love me, why do you whip me?

1538. Daddy said Son, I can't explain it. If I had to get it, you must too.

1539. Today's parents possess dripping blood on their hands, because they have spared the rod for the spoiling of the child.

1540. The Word of God says, love one another as He has loved us.

1541. Our yea, may be a nay. Our nay, may be a yea. Times are no longer the same.

1542. Wrong once was right. Now, right has become a wrong.

1543. What use to be, ain't no more. Times have changed.

1544. The Word of God says, there is beauty in Holiness.

1545. As a people of color, we must learn to strive together for a bigger and better democracy, which flows from the lowest valley to the highest mountains for all mankind.

1546. Once a Black Person deescalate fear within a group of Whites, the atmosphere takes on a change of persuasion.

1547. There is always a White fearfulness hidden somewhere underneath of Black Folk.

1548. God is calling your name, because you are somewhere naked in the garden.

1549. With the Lord, nothing happens in the past or future; only in the present do things happen. He is the presence of things and time.

1550. Our thoughts must remain in the presence of the Lord; not the past nor future.

1551. God's presence resides in our presence at all time. Do not let your mind overrule.

1552. Our minds must have a divine spiritual discernment for the betterment our lives.

1553. Too often, we sit on our do nothing butts; to include sitting on the Lord all the time.

1554. Ain't no handouts in His line. He said, occupy till, I come. Otherwise, stay busy.

1555. Passive people very seldom achieve the dreams which have been prescribed to them.

1556. Avoid the looking back demeanor of Lot's wife; good purpose awaits inside of you now.

1557. The former things will stagnate you.

1558. The past will keep you stuck in neutral.

1559. Divorce the old stuff out of your mind and Spirit.

1560. The wrong Demon will possess you enough to love somebody that don't even love you.

1561. Yes, life does have many miscalculations which tends to stiffen us.

1562. Busy people stay busy. Busy people place more and more challenges onto their plates.

1563. Lord, enlarge my territory to be Blessed and Highly Favored beyond the imaginable.

1564. God's Blessings are irrevocable through His Promises and the declaration of our Amen.

1565. This day shall be a manifestation of His Promises upon you.

1566. When Jesus called His Disciples, He made a callout only for boys that were busy working.

1567. We must be broken and contrite in order to hear God speak; He breaks in order to do surgery on us.

1568. The Glory of God burns to retrieve our attention and call. Ask Moses about his burning.

1569. Let the Lord call you out. Congregate some trees together in the woods, to "*whom*" you can preach the Word of God.

1570. Never lower our God to your level; we must rise to His level. His ways are not our ways.

1571. God's Word can never be fully fulfilled in our lives as long as we watch different media sources as being Gospel.

1572. In this life, we must learn to pay more attention to deescalating the stresses of daily living.

1573. We can't predict the things which can't be predicted.

1574. Don't say you were led by the Spirit when you know beyond a shadow of doubt, you were led by emotions. Emotions will not give vent to the Spirit.

1575. God always does more than what we have asked of Him in our prayers. Go back and reconcile your answered prayers.

1576. Let's hold fast to the profession of our Faith in Christ Jesus.

1577. Worship is a mind stayed on Jesus; fasten, locked-in and steadfast.

1578. Have you been tipping out on the Lord lately?

1579. There are various types of Demons affecting various types of people; looking for your most concerned venue.

1580. Demons are parasites to human existence. They attack in various ways of human existence. The body, mind, Spirit and physical existence.

1581. Not only is Satan a Mayhem, but he is a "*Demon Demiser.*" Yes, Demis-er.

1582. Sick and tired of being sick and tired has become a way of life in the neighborhood.

1583. Success is the measurement of the affected outcome desired.

1584. Loan a church member some money and you are guaranteed to have another enemy.

1585. If you run after honor, honor will run from you.

1586. Ask Joseph, the one who possessed a coat of many colors...We must go through Hell to rule in Heavenly places.

1587. Even though, Joseph had sense enough to run like hell.

1588. There was a day and time, when little Black girls played with White Baby dolls.

1589. He sits high; yet, looks low; in the midst of His looking, you are inclusive.

1590. Avoid letting other folk push your buttons. Press your own buttons at your own dispensation.

1591. Let your toilet be your Situation Room, where there shall be no political oversight.

1592. Let your toilet be the place where you can take everything to the Lord in prayer.

1593. There is a Blessing in your pressing.

1594. The rabbit boast about winning the race against the turtle. Well, the turtle kept pressing, while the rabbit thought he could take a quick nap along the way. Now, you know the rest of the story.

1595. Jesus, LIFESAVER.

1596. Oh, it is Jesus, *"passin"* by; I decide to give Him a try.

1597. Yes, Jesus came as an imaginary gift; a gift unto His own. His own received Him not.

1598. Goodness and Mercy will take us into Eternity.

1599. Life is not to be understood, but withstood. Ask Job for his consensus.

1600. The one thing Job discovered about his search of life was the realness of a living God.

1601. Our world has become desensitized beyond healing.

1602. Our love for one another as a people of color has waxed too cold with desensitization.

1603. Limited immunity does not cover for our Sins. Only His Blood for the remission of Sin.

1604. Don't sell out your Black to the highest bidder.

1605. Don't be so hard on yourself; it ain't what you have done, but it's what you are doing.

1606. Know where you stand with the Lord. Don't fool yourself.

1607. You can't be jacked-up in your cares and have Faith in Jesus at the same time.

1608. Lord, I am pressing my way everyday all the way.

1609. Lord, I pray you exalt me above all the extremities of this life.

1610. There is nothing about me worth my being about me.

1611. Time itself has nothing to do with time.

1612. Time does not restrict itself.

1613. Time is not of essence.

1614. Time has no restrictions.

1615. Only the Lord knows time.

1616. Neither the Son of Man, nor the Angels know time.

1617. He is the Beginning and the End.

1618. He never ever works in the past nor future; only in the present.

1619. He knows the end before the end.

1620. *"Had you been here, my brother would have not died."*

1621. We possess misappropriated stresses for no reason. Ask Mary and Martha.

1622. Sickness, dying and death along with time.....does not constraint the Lord.

1623. On a dying bed, nothing matters except life on earth or life in Heaven.

1624. We constraint ourselves, because of our ignorance of who the Lord is in our lives.

1625. We are guilty of making grievous mandates upon the Lord.

1626. Again, it has been said, relying on your past will keep you stuck in neutral.

1627. He only works in the present; ask Lazarus. Then ask Mary and Martha.

1628. God's intention was not to heal him, but to raise him from the dead as an answer to Job's question that was caught in the cloud. If a man die, shall he live again?

1629. Lazarus' death was subrogated by the Almighty Himself, to the present moment.

1630. He resurrected Lazarus with a new and whole body.

1631. He had two deaths and three opportunities at life.

1632. He surpassed healing by making him new and whole apart from his sickness and death.

1633. He is an on time God. Yes, He is...Never too late. Ask Mary and Martha.

1634. God's people of color perish for a lack of knowledge.

1635. God's people of color perish for a lack of obedience with no longing for knowledge.

1636. Satan has DEAD or ALIVE wanted posters out on all the Saints. Tread lite wherever you go.

1637. BEWARE: Satan does whatever he can do to make it harder for Believers.

1638. His hellish desire is to steal your personal identity for his gain. He goes to and fro seeking.

1639. He is a cyber seeking. He is a "*stanking spywarrior.*"

1640. Think it not strange, when ye fall into divers temptations; better known as Evilness.

1641. Momma said, there will be days like "*this.*"

1642. We are His People and the Sheep of His Pasture.

1643. In His presence, we move and have our being.

1644. Your character is how God sees you.

1645. The love of Jesus just wants to hear your cry.

1646. Due time is all it takes for the Lord to rescue a Sin-Sick-Soul.

1647. Aren't you glad the Lord saved you from a dying Hell?

1648. One day, all of us will be headed to the great beyond. There won't be a Democrat or Republican, Black or White. Ultimately, there will be a Heaven or Hell waiting.

1649. Blessed and Highly Favored. Avoid flaunting the favor which God has given you.

1650. Round nine, down, but ain't out. We fall down, but *"us"* get up.

1651. Death can only defeat me for a little while, but the grave has to let me go.

1652. People of God, a forged master plan has been designed for all mankind. It's *"Bout"* ready for us to catch the morning train; evening train may be too late.

1653. The past and future is for man's records, but God yet works in the present tense.

1654. The Lord works in the now and not the then or should have been.

1655. In the reservoir of my mind, I can hear the old chant..."*Down through the years, the Lord has been good to me.*"

1656. Through many dangers, toils and snares...We have already come with cracks in our Black.

1657. Don't feel no ways tired; come too far from whence I started.

1658. If we ever find ourselves pressing a prolonging dying pillow, give Him the praise anyhow.

1659. God never takes away, where He does not promise to add. Ask Job.

1660. Our sufferings of this world have charted the courses of life like a hurricane on the ocean's waters.

1661. If all you see is the gravy on the table, Believe Him for the steak too.

1662. The presence of the Lord is up in this here place.

1663. In bereavement, leaving is better than staying; to die is gain.

1664. In a dying hour, I will praise Him anyhow.

1665. Until death takes its behold in that hour of departure.

1666. God's will must be done.

1667. Then, I can read my title clear to the mansion in the sky; I bid farewell to every fear.

1668. When I see Jesus, say Amen.

1669. Life is as a vapor; it soon dissipates.

1670. Our Soul is forever longing to return to her Maker.

1671. This book, "The Civil Rights of Black Theology," along with the Word of God, maybe your Salvation for hope; to include hope for your Salvation.

1672. Jesus will leave the light on for you.

1673. Yet, death cannot keep me and the grave cannot hold me.

1674. O' Death where is thou sting? O' Grave where is thou victory?

1675. I shall see Him for myself, by and by.

1676. And all God's People say, Amen.

1677. With an ugly look on his face, this little black boy shouted to his teachers, the cafeteria needs a cookbook.

PRAYER OF THE BLACK CHURCH

Guide me, O thou Great Jehovah, Pilgrim through this

barren land: I am weak, but thou art Mighty, hold me

with thy powerful hand: Bread of Heaven, Bread of Heaven,

Feed me till I want

no more.

AMEN

PROVERBIAL ESSENTIALS FOR BLACK LIVING IV

Proverbial Four has been extracted from various portions of the book, "War on the Saints" by Jessie Penn-Lewis. For all persons seeking freedom from the power of Satan and his Imps, these excerpts have been extracted for your spiritual benefit:

"Keep claiming the power of the Blood."

"Pray for light and face the past."

"Never give up hope."

"Avoid all self-introspection."

"Live and pray for others, and thus keep your Spirit in full aggressive and resisting power." (Resisting the power of Satan)

"Use your mind, and THINK-think over all you do, and say, are."

"Live in the moment, watch and pray step by step."

"Decide for yourself in everything you can. Do not lean on others."

"Take the initiative, instead of passively depending on others."

"Act as far as you can, doing what you can."

"Refuse and reject all lies and excuses, as they are recognized."

"I Choose the Will God, and refuse the will of Satan."

"A great victory means great danger, because when the believer is occupied with it, the Devil is scheming how to rob him of it. The hour of victory therefore calls for soberness of mind, and watching unto prayer for a little over elation may mean its loss and a long sore fight back to full victory."

"Refusal of all ground to Evil Spirits."

"If the believer is conscious of a weight on his Spirit, he must get rid of the weight by refusing all the *"causes"* of the weight; for it is necessary to keep the Spirit unburdened to fight, and to retain power of detection."

"Demons long for bodies to possess."

Non-Believers are open to the following deceptions

"Open to lies, through ignorance; unrighteousness through ignorance."

"Divisions and quarrels."

"Reckless unwatchfulness."

"Doubt and unbelief."

"Relying on reason instead of God's Word."

"Relying on work without prayer."

PROVERBIAL ESSENTIALS FOR BLACK LIVING V

PRAYERS OF DIVINE DISPENSATION

Father God, Your handy hand has shown us through the scriptures how sickness, dying and death were dealt with in the life of the Woman with the issue of blood. Her sickness was for twelve long years. Lord, we saw how You dealt with Jarius' daughter at the tender age of twelve years old. Yet, Lazarus was sick unto death, but by the hollow of Your most powerful feet, death was treaded down. **Amen.**

Lord, with all that has befallen Your people, through the darkness of recent days, still we come with a praise painted upon our lips in spite of our struggles with sickness, dying and death. We have declared the New Normal, which shall be Jesus the Christ, even the more. **Amen.**

Father God, In the midst of these uncertain times, we know the thief comes to steal, kill and destroy. The meditations of our prayers shall echo thru the chords of our voices; through the pulsations of our hearts, that God Himself, shall see us through the darkness of day. **Amen.**

Lord, "We shall sing that song full of Faith which our dark past has taught us. God of our weary years; God of our silent tears; thou who has brought us thus far on the way." **Amen.**

Dear Lord, Your people are yet tired along the way; weary and worn from the stresses of the New Normal. Let us rest our troubled hearts upon the slate of Your bosom, where You promised sweet rest for our weary Souls. Let it be Lord, even the more; forever and ever. **Amen.**

Father God, the Old Saints would say, "You been good by us." Likewise, we have come to declare the power of Your Goodness over ourselves. Have Your way concerning us, Lord. Continue the dispensation of Your Goodness, even the more. **Amen.**

Our Prayer Lord: Dispense what you have purchased for Your people; "Inspite" of "Black Lives" being lost by hellish assaults through the etching Evils of a Sinful world. **Amen.**

Yes Lord, it's time for a change; to begin in me; to begin in others. Our weeping has endured for a season. **Amen.**

Ain't nothing NEW...Let it be known, every night before bed, I "TAKE THE KNEE." These are my words...Father, now, I lay me down to sleep, Bless my Soul to keep, if I should die before I wake, I pray thee Lord, my Soul to take. If I should live for another day, I pray the Lord, guide me along the way. **Amen.**

God of our weary years.
God of our silent tears.
Thou who has brought us thus far on the way. **Amen.**

Your people are yet tired along the way; weary and worn from the stresses of the New Normal. Let us rest our troubled hearts upon the slate of Your bosom, where You promised sweet rest for our weary Souls. Let it be Lord, even the more; forever and ever, **Amen.**

Dear God, because we are Yours and belong to You, ONLY... Now, we pray over our being, that You may be Glorified. We submit this our prayer in the Name of Christ. **Amen.**

Lord, we pray that Your righteousness become a pervasive power to overcome this present day pandemic which has come against the well-being of Your people. You are the Mighty God. We stand not in the fate of fear, but in the realm of Faith, that You may receive all Glory and Honor, in the Beloved Name of Jesus, Your Son. **Amen.**

Lord, we come reposed before Your presence to say, thank you; that our beds were not our cooling boards last night. Yet, we come anyhow. We speak over ourselves that deliverance would cover us in the midst of this present day Evil; For Thine is the Power, the Glory and the Honor, in the Name of Jesus, the Christ, we pray. **Amen.**

Father God in Heaven, we find ourselves as living prospect, stuck between the realms of sickness, dying and death. Yet, we know that You still rule and super rule with all power, yet in the palms of Your Almighty Hands. Father, there is no room for sickness, dying and death in the lives of Your people...as we pray, in the Beloved and Bountiful Name of Jesus the Christ. **Amen.**

Father God in Heaven, thank you for sustaining us thus far in these trying times of uncertainty. Yet, we are confident that this too shall pass, as we navigate our lives through the prospects of everyday living. Now Lord, we will be ever so careful to give You all the praise, all the Glory and all the Honor...In the Name of Jesus, we submit this our prayer. **Amen.**

Our Father God, life has become a query of uncertainties. Lord, ain't nothing we can do except pray; a roller coaster ride, with ups and downs, curves and straights. Yet, we abide in the Shadow of Your Glory, that we may make it, to see what the end is going to be like, as we pray, in the Beloved Name of Him , who died for us; Jesus the Christ. **Amen.**

Father God in Heaven, Bless each day which comes before us and each night that comes behind us, that we may be sufficed by the shadow of Your Glory; that our living be not in vain; we pray over ourselves for Your dispensations of courage, hope, and strength. Be our God and we shall be Your people, as we pray, even the more. **Amen.**

Lord help us along this way. The journey is tedious, as Momma would say. Under the sound of this my weak voice, there is a waiting congregation. Continue to do good by us Lord, as we shall do good by You. Let us not tread down Your Grace by the hollow of our Sinful feet; as You deliver us from Evil....for Thine is the Kingdom, the Power and the Glory, Forever, **Amen.**

Father God, we come before You this morning to make mention of Your most Holy Name and to call upon Your Righteousness as God. You are worthy to be praised as we seek You out for this day; not Your handy hand, but Your Glory; that it may be revealed in our lives... As we pray now in the Name of Jesus our Lord and His most Righteous Name. **Amen.**

When seconds matter the most, it's not who you can call, but it's who you call on. His Name is Jesus, the Captain of our Salvation. Father God, with expressions of love and gratitude, we come calling upon Your Name, because every second of everyday, life does matter, as we are praying in the most Beloved Name of Him who died for us, Jesus the Christ. **Amen.**

Our Father God in Heaven, we come as recipients of Your morning invocation, that Blessings may be instilled upon each of us for this day; we pray in the most Beloved name of Him who died for us, Jesus the Christ. **Amen.**

Lord, we look unto the hills, not just unto the hills, but unto Your Most Holy Hills to be Blessed of You and Your Most Holy Righteousness. **Amen.**

Lord, counsel us through the reins of our minds. **Amen.**

Father God, thank You for authoring and writing Your people into this day with a purpose and plan; waking us up and starting us on a new day with a portion of health and strengthen. We were robed in our right minds with the activities of our limbs. As Momma would say Lord, "nobody, but the Lord". Subro-

gate us through this day that Your Glory may be revealed in our lives. **Amen.**

Pray with me. Lord, we have come to make mention of Your Most Holy and Righteous name; still, we anticipate Your endowed Blessings upon each of our lives in this most unpredictable season, when life has become so uncertain. Yet, we trust You for the outcome and the worth of prayer through the dispensation of Your Grace. In the Name of Christ, we make utterance. **Amen.**

Bow with me. Our Father God in Heaven, we come as recipients of Your morning invocation that Blessings shall be instilled upon each of us for this day. Catch us by the reins of our minds, while we pray the revelation of Your Glory to be revealed. As we press our way in the Name of Jesus, the Christ, we pray. **Amen.**

Lord God, if You will, give us a jump start into this new day, which has been set before us, as we have come to Bless You by the way of prayer. Make good our living that Your Glory may be revealed; that men, women, boys and girls would have known that we have been with You. In the name of Him, Who died for all mankind, Jesus the Christ. **Amen.**

Our Father God in Heaven, we come as recipients of your morning invocation for our lives that Blessings shall be instilled upon us for this day, without exclusions. Catch us by the reins of our minds, while we pray the revelation of Your Glory to be revealed. Now, as we press our way in the Most Beloved of

Him, Jesus the Christ. **Amen.**

Lord God, be the coffee and tea in our cups; the milk and juice in our glasses and the water in our bottles, as we seek You out for this Blessed day. Still, we anticipate Blessings upon our lives. Yet, we still trust You for all things; health, wealth, peace and prosperity to come as we live in these most uncertain times. This is our prayer of Hope, as we pray now. Jesus, **Amen.**

We come this morning Lord seeking Your favor, forgiveness, Goodness and Grace; to include health and healing with tender mercies. We petition for the bounty of Your peace and pros-perity upon our lives by the fullness of Your Glorious dispensa-tion, as we pray the prayer of Faith. Jesus, **Amen.**

No more my Lord, No more! After being verbally abused by his father all of his childhood during the late 1800's, he was brought to the cotton field and told to start picking. After as-sessing the situation of how massive the field and nobody else to help pick cotton, he immediately waited for his father to leave the field. Then and then only, he made another assess-ment of the situation. Thus, he whispered a prayer and turned the cotton basket upside down on a fence post. He declared to himself by saying, No More My Lord, No More! He ran with due diligence like a runaway slave. Years later, after becoming a grown man, he returned to his father's house for a son-to-father visit. This has been a true story with the fragrance of a hearty, **Amen.**

PROVERBIAL ESSENTIALS FOR BLACK LIVING VI

Just to paraphrase, know where you sit on the continuum of compassion to judgement. There is a continuum by which you must first be judged. Judge not, that ye be not judged. Judgement of ourselves lead to less judgement of those around us. Judgement is define as *"as an opinion or opinions treated as facts."* It is felt that some of us need to self-assess ourselves and come to grips with life by means of compassion, empathy and less judgement. Our judgement cannot and should not be categorized as a misfortune, calamity or divine punishment upon others. Make judgement of self, before judgement of others befall the infiltration of your most *"Holy"* character.

PROVERBIAL ESSENTIALS FOR BLACK LIVING VII

PORTAL OF POETRY

"LEAVE YOUR PROBLEMS AT THE DOOR"

If you have problems.....I know, we all do.

The only thing wanted is survival enough to get through.

But here is a simple solution which you can use more, more and more.

When things overwhelm you, leave your problems at the door.

When people are around you, nagging on, on, and on.

Visitors are coming in and out while you are yelling, WILL SOMEBODY GET THAT PHONE!

Don't let people stress you out and things become an uproar.

Just smile and keep going, but leave those problems at the door.

Somebody's bad attitude has gotten you bent all out of shape.

Now, you are upset; you feel like you just cannot escape.

The day keeps dragging you down to the core.

Don't you fret, there is hope for you.

Yet, leave those problems at the door.

You want to smile on the outside, but your inside is filled with unnecessary mess.

It is like a painful toothache with an overgrown abscess.

Taking all that drama, discontentment and so much more.

Be a happier you, but leave those problems at the door.

There is so much to be gained from joy within the earth.

You are somebody who deserves happiness and for all it's worth.

Don't walk around being bitter, be a better you than ever before.

Close your eyes, exhale and breathe, but leave those problems at the door.

Position yourself to receive.

Pray about it and Believe.

Prepare your mind to implore.

Problematic situations need to be left at the door.

By Barbara R. Wells

PROVERBIAL ESSENTIALS FOR BLACK LIVING VIII

If my Mother was here today, these are the words my Mother would say...

If my Father was here today, these are the words my Father would say...

Father, I stretch my hand to thee. No other help I know.

He heard my cries; pitied my every groan.

He bowed His ear and chased my grief away.

Let my heart no more despair, while I have breath to pray and sigh.

He beheld me, sore distressed; He bade my pains away.

Return my Soul to God, thy rest.

Yes, I *"wanna"* go where Jesus is...I *"wanna"* go there too.

I am bound for Mount Zion. Way out on a hill.

Come by here Dear Lord, somebody's praying.

This maybe my last time, I don't know. Maybe, the last time we sing and shout again.

"Gonna" lay down my burdens, down by the riverside.

To study war no more.

When I get home, how happy, I will be. When I get home, my Saviour's face I'll see.

I'll never more shall roam. The bells will be ringing, the Saints will be singing, when I get home.

EPILOGUE

Black Theology is what has kept people of color sane for the last four hundred years, until now. Throughout generations, we have been a people who has been segregated by plantation plots, names of streets, subdivisions, train tracks, and physical boundaries such as waterways.

The same question has been asked throughout generations with a pending reply; caught between here and yonder with a wonder still lurking. "The Matter Wit Me?" We are a Holy People; set aside by a Holy God. We are Americas' democracy and salvation; even though we have backslidden, due to the feigned perks allocated by the White populous. Yet, we still strive for rightful citizenship as Americans, while in the midst of a 2021 voters' suppression.

Black America has been crippled with lameness, because of constant injustices imposed by the fading majority. The populous have failed to realize that imposed hate accumulates other social problems with affecting consequences. Black Theology fends for itself through the liberation of the oppressed. A theology which empowers through prayer, preaching and musical interpretations; to include ring shouts from the Mother Land. The theology of the populous avoids speaking of the oppressed within sermonic discourses.

Black Folk refuted the ideology of White Christianity, because of Black oppression.

How can Christianity oppress a people of God? Thus, Black Theology migrated into the dwelling place of Black Souls, which empowered one to deny White Christianity and place his trust the Living God of all Mankind.

White theology has overlooked the shadows of oppression posed upon a people of color. It should be a preached and practiced theology which exemplifies, mitigates, and arbitrate for Black Humanity on a large scale for a common society in which all men are created equal and shall be treated equal. Yet, civil laws attempt to dictate what theology should have taught. Everything about the White mission field and her missionaries have everything to do with rectifying and restoring Black Humanity into the hearing and hearts of her people.

The Civil Rights of Black Theology is a common sense theology embedded from our past. A birthed theology from enslavement, which caused an exertion to manifest within a people to endure with the crisis of hope regardless of the circumstances.

"What shall we do with the Negro?" Regardless of what has been done, we have been able to enjoy some of the amenities which are possessed in the American experience. A theology which identifies Jesus as the Battle Axe; the God of the oppressed and downtrodden with a hope for tomorrow. We too, were despised and rejected; yet, He was acquainted with all our griefs and sorrows.

The hem of His garment became the symbol of hope for the downtrodden. We are a people which has been empowered to resist, yet to engage.

As Black Folk, just because He Lives, we can face-all-fear. Just because He Lives, we can face tomorrow with whatever it shall bring.

Yes! Deep in our hearts, we do Believe, we shall overcome.

"The Lord Bless us and keep us; the Lord make His face to shine upon us, and be gracious unto us.

The Lord lift up His countenance upon us, and grant us peace." Amen.

BIOGRAPHICAL SURVEY OF THE AUTHOR

When Dwight Eisenhower held the office, President of the United States of America, needless to say, I was born into a color bias society filled with poverty and segregation. These were the days of Colored Folks, Black maids for White folks, back of the bus, Colored schools and institutions for Colored learning, no checkbooks, no charge cards, poverty, rationed government commodities, filling stations, telephone books, transistor radios, no televisions and outdoor toilets. The days when you borrowed meal, flour, sugar and whatever else from the next door neighbor to make ends meet. I am now at the age of sixty-seven years old with adoptive and biological children. My parents could not and did not receive a formal education, but had what Black Folks called, common sense; to include wisdom with a dash of *"Mother Wit."* I must admit, life was good to us, except for the shadows of the Jim Crow theology, which was imposed and passed down through generations of the Black Experience.

My Father believed in education as the primary key to being above the norm in society. He made sure the ethics of education and hard work played a major role in my life. He inspired me from the past portals of his childhood, where life was filled with an onslaught of challenges. On the other hand, my Mother inspired me with creativity of the mind through the worth of being above the average. Each of my parents designed a virtual mainstay in my life, which I have passed onto my children.

I enrolled in college while being gainfully employed and maneuvered my way through to the achievement of a Master of Theology. The Black Experience gave way to empowering my skillset of reaching into Black neighborhoods to plant churches and establish outreaches; to include adopting and fostering the deserving and underprivileged.

Most conclusive, I have lived through the days of protests and riots; still, the way has not been easy, but a path was left for me to find and follow. After it is all said and done, I must salute Rosa Parks for leaving a seat in the front of the bus for a little Black fellow, like myself. Yet, through my rigid childhood mentoring and training, I have overcome the stigma of being Black without hope in a White society.

J. O. Gatson, Th.M
jgatson1@bellsouth.net

NOTES & RESOURCES

King James Version of the Bible

"United Negro College Fund" Theme Script

The Baptist Hymnal, New Edition 1920, The American Baptist Publication Society, Judson Press

National Primitive Baptist Hymn Book, Printed by National Primitive Baptist Publishing Board, January, 1964

"Gospel Pearls" by the Music Committee, Sunday School Publishing Board, National Baptist Convention, U S A, Nashville Tennessee

"God of the Oppressed" by James H. Cone, Published 1975
ISBN 1-57075-158-7, Seabury Press

"Open Season" by Ben Crump, Copyright 2019
ISBN 978-0-06-237509-4, Harper Collins, page 49

"The Black National Anthem" James Weldon Johnson & J. Rosamond Johnson

"War On The Saints" by Jessie Penn-Lewis in collaboration with Evan Roberts (Printed in the United States of America, First American Edition 1977, edition by special arrangement with the British publishers: The Overcomer Literature Trust 3 Munster Road, Parkstone, Poole, Dorset, BH14 9PS England   pages 98, 99, 134, 138, 141

"The Ministry of Music In The Black Church" by J. Wendall Mapson, Jr., Copyright 1984
ISBN 0-8170-1057-2, Judson Press, page 15, 41, 85

"The MASTER" by John Pollock, Copyright 1984
ISBN 0-89693-315-6, Victor Books, pages 203, 212

Made in the USA
Columbia, SC
19 June 2023

17949201R10150